Best
TEA SHOP WALKS
IN HAMPSHIRE

Margaret and Barrie Howard

Published by Sigma Leisure – an imprint of
Sigma Press, 1 South Oak Lane, Wilmslow, Cheshire SK9 6AR, England.

British Library Cataloguing in Publication Data
A CIP record for this book is available from the British Library.

ISBN: 1-85058-621-7

Typesetting and Design by: Sigma Press, Wilmslow, Cheshire.

Cover: Wherwell village

Maps and photographs: the authors

Printed by: MFP Design and Print

Contents

Introduction   **1**

    Tea Shops   3

    The Walks   4

    Public Transport   5

The Walks

1. Winchester & St Catherine's Hill   **6**

     Distance: 4½ miles.

2. New Alresford   **12**

     Distance: 6 miles.

3. Chawton & Upper Farringdon   **17**

     Distance: 5 miles.

4. Selborne Hanger   **22**

     Distance: 5½ miles.

5. Petersfield and Ashford Hanger   **27**

     Distance: 7½ miles.

6. Buriton & Queen Elizabeth Country Park   **32**

     Distance: 8 miles.

7. Rowlands Castle   37
Distance: 4 miles.

8. Hambledon & Broadhalfpenny Down   41
Distance: 6½ miles.

9. Wickham and The Forest of Bere   46
Distance: 5¼ miles.

10. Bishop's Waltham   51
Distance: 6 miles.

11. Botley & Manor Farm Country Park   56
Distance: 4¾ miles.

12. Hamble & The Royal Victoria Country Park   61
Distance: 5¾ miles.

13. Exbury and The Solent   65
Distance: 5¾ miles.

14. Milford-on-Sea. Keyhaven & Hurst Castle   69
Distance: 7 miles (6 miles if not taking the ferry).

15. Brockenhurst and Aldridge Hill Inclosure   74
Distance: 5¼ miles.

16. Holmsley, Wilverley Inclosure and The Naked Man   78
Distance: 5¾ miles.

17. Burley & Whitten Pond   83
Distance: 5 miles.

18. Acres Down and Holidays Hill Inclosure 87

Distance: 6¾ miles.

19. Minstead and The Rufus Stone 93

Distance: 5 miles.

20. Fordingbridge & The Avon Valley Path 98

Distance: 6½ miles.

21. Breamore Manor & Rockbourne 103

Distance: 7 miles.

22. The Water Ways of Romsey 108

Distance: 6 miles.

23. Mottisfont & Spearywell Wood 113

Distance: 6 miles.

24. Longstock, Danebury Hill & Stockbridge 118

Distance: 7½ miles.

25. Wherwell, Goodworth Clatford & Chilbolton 123

Distance: 8½ miles.

26. Whitchurch & Freefolk 128

Distance: 5¼ miles.

Summary of Walks

Walk	Location	Distance	Teashop	Description
1	Winchester	4½ miles	Cathedral Refectory. Wide choice.	Easy after a steep climb at start. Riverside, meadows, historic city. Lovely views.
2	New Alresford	6 miles	Traditional. Further choice.	Strenuous. Undulating fields, ascending tracks, riverside. Steam railway. Good views.
3	Chawton	5 miles	Traditional.	Easy. Meadows, woods. Jane Austen's home.
4	Selborne	5½ miles	Traditional. Further choice.	Strenuous. Two short woodland climbs, undulating fields. Superb views.
5	Petersfield	7½ miles	Traditional. Further choice.	Strenuous. Hampshire Hangers, steep ascents & descents. Splendid views.
6	Buriton	8 miles	Country Park Visitor Centre café.	Strenuous. Steep climbs through woods & fields. Country Park. Iron-age settlement. Lovely views.
7	Rowlands Castle	4 miles	Traditional.	Easy. Undulating meadows, light woodland. Good views.
8	Hambledon	6½ miles	Village store teashop.	Moderate. Meadows, woods, gentle ascents. Splendid views.
9	Wickham	5¼ miles	Antique Centre. Further choice.	Moderate. Undulating woods, open commons. Can be muddy.
10	Bishop's Waltham	6 miles	Traditional. Further choice.	Moderate. Woods, meadows. Two gentle ascents. Splendid views. Palace ruins.
11	Botley	4¾ miles	Converted barn in traditional farm. Further Choice in Botley.	Easy. Riverside, fields, woods. Country Park and working farm museum.
12	Hamble	5¾ miles	Traditional. Country Park café *en route*.	Easy. Some road walking, fields, coast, Country Park, river estuary. Fine views.
13	Exbury	5¾ miles	Converted blacksmith forge. Country Park café *en route*.	Easy. Meadows, light woodland, coast. Country Park, Exbury Gardens. Superb views.

Walk	Location	Distance	Teashop	Description
14	Milford-on-Sea	7 miles	Seafront café. Traditional in town.	Easy. Fields, woods, coast. Ferry trip to Hurst Castle. Splendid views.
15	Brockenhurst New Forest	5¼ miles	Traditional.	Moderate. Heathland, woodland & streams. Extensive views.
16	Holmsley New Forest	5¾ miles	Converted railway station.	Moderate. Riverside, forest, heathland. Superb views. Can be muddy.
17	Burley New Forest	5 miles	Traditional. Further choice.	Moderate. Undulating heathland. Splendid views.
18	Acres Down New Forest	6¾ miles	Farmhouse.	Moderate. Undulating heathland, forest, Knightwood Oak, Reptiliary. Superb views.
19	Minstead New Forest	5 miles	Traditional.	Moderate. Forest, Rufus Stone, Furzey Gardens.
20	Fordingbridge & New Forest	6½ miles	Traditional. Further choice in town.	Moderate. Fields, heathland, water meadows. Superb views.
21	Breamore	7 miles	Converted barn at Breamore Manor.	Moderate. Undulating downland, ascending woods, picturesque village, mizmaze. Superb views.
22	Romsey	6 miles	Interesting choice in town. Garden Centre *en route*.	Easy. Fields, woods, riverside, towpath. A little road-walking. Historic city.
23	Mottisfont	6 miles	Village Post Office.	Moderate. Woods, meadows, riverside. Mottisfont Abbey (NT).
24	Longstock	7½ miles	Traditional. Further choice.	Strenuous. Ascending tracks, undulating fields, hillfort. Beautiful landscape, splendid views.
25	Wherwell	8½ miles	Traditional.	Moderate. Meadows, woods, riverside. Links three picturesque villages. Some road-walking.
26	Whitchurch	5¼ miles	In working silk mill.	Easy. Meadows, farm tracks, riverside. Beautiful landscape.

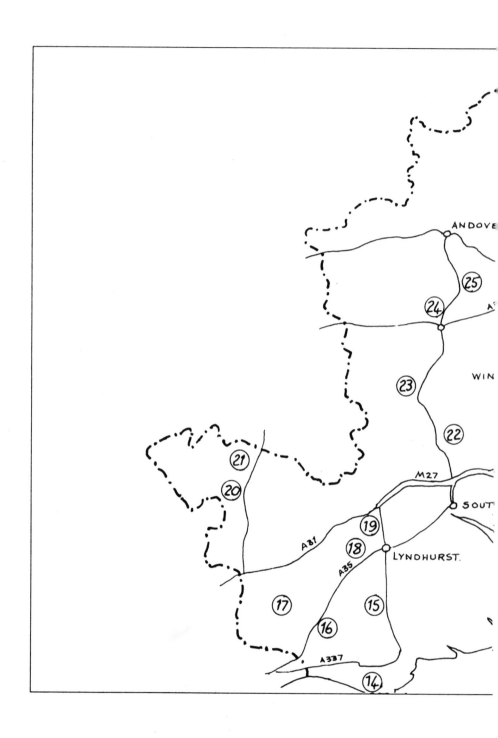

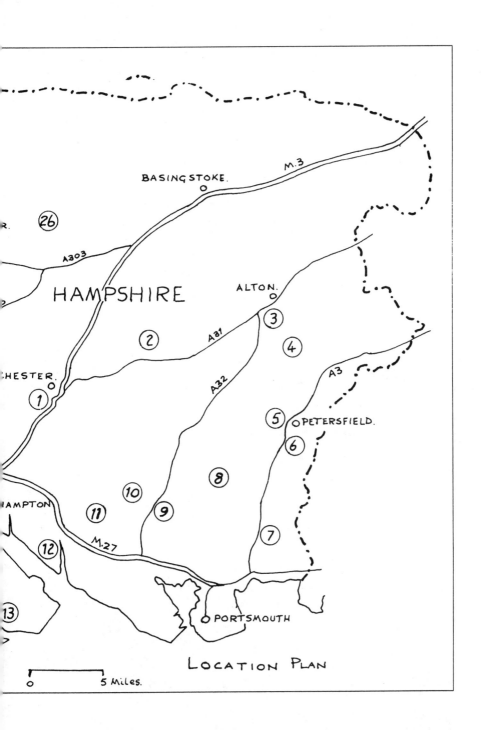

LOCATION PLAN

0 ____ 5 Miles.

KEY TO SYMBOLS USED ON SKETCH MAPS

Path on route	- - - →
Path not on route	• • • •
Road	═══
River	∿∿∿∿
Pond, lake or sea	≈≈≈
Church	+
Tea Shop	T
Trig. point	△
Car Park	C.P.
Public House	P.H
View point	_⋆_
Building referred to in text	▬
Windmill	⋔
Point in text	②
Railway	┼┼┼┼

Introduction

A walk in rural Hampshire is an exploration of one of the prettiest and most varied counties in the country. Myriad footpaths lead over gentle rolling downland and moorland; through ancient woods and idyllic thatched villages; along clear, free-flowing rivers and the southern coastline.

Central to Hampshire is the ancient and royal City of Winchester, the capital of Alfred the Great's Kingdom of Wessex. Winchester's Old Minster was where William the Conqueror held a triumphal second coronation, a few weeks after his first at London. It was in Winchester Castle that the Domesday Survey was stored and the Treasury and Exchequer developed. However, the city is not only historic; it is also a place of exceptional beauty. William Cobbett said in 1830, 'Here are hill, dell, water, meadows ... and all of them very fine and beautiful.' More than 150 years later this is still true.

The Hampshire Downs, a continuation of Salisbury Plain, sweep across the county eastward as far as the North and South Downs of Surrey and Sussex. Along their northern boundary they plunge down to the Kennet and Thames valleys. Southwards they give way to the gentle sandy landscape of the Hampshire Basin. Seventeen miles of the South Downs are in Hampshire: St Catherine's Hill (walk 1) at a height of 100 metres (328ft) and the best place to view Winchester from, is its last hill; Butser Hill (walk 6) at 270 metres (888ft), is the highest point throughout its entire length.

The chalk downland and fields provide habitat for an exciting diversity of flora and fauna: orchid, gentian, scabious, harebell, vetch, cowslip and the common rock-rose all flourish and in turn support a variety of butterflies including the Adonis Blue, the Chalkhill Blue and the Silver-Spotted Skipper. Birds of the chalkland scrub are grasshopper warbler, yellowhammer and linnet. As you cross the open fields you may hear, as we did, the lovely song of the skylark.

Meandering gently through peaceful valleys and delightful thatched villages, the Hampshire rivers have a charm and tranquillity seldom found elsewhere. The Test, Itchen, Meon and Avon are commonly known as chalk streams: water filters through the dry chalk upland to break out, crystal clear, at the foot of the hills. The

Test and Itchen flow into Southampton Water; the Meon into The Solent and the Avon crosses the western end of the county into the English Channel at Christchurch.

Over the centuries these rivers have provided power for the turning of many mill wheels. The Itchen was once part navigable; its route can still be seen below St Catherine's Hill. The clear, chalk-washed free-flowing Test and Itchen have long been famous for their association with fishing for salmon, trout and grayling; the Test has been said to be the most famous fishing river in all England. The beauty of the rivers is enhanced by the variety of plants along the riverbanks: yellow flag iris, mimulus – the monkey flower, Himalayan balsam, purple loosestrife and the unrelated yellow loosestrife are but a few to be seen in their seasons.

The Rivers Beaulieu, Hamble, Avon Water and Lymington all have their sources in the heathland of the Hampshire Basin. In the 18th century, the Lymington was used by vessels supplying salt to most of southern England and exporting as far as America. Production raised to 4000 tons per year by 1800; however, the industry fell into decline by the 1860s due to the high cost of coal used in the furnaces for boiling the sea water. Today these rivers are popular yachting centres.

Bucklers Hard, on the River Beaulieu was renowned for shipbuilding. Between 1745 and 1822, seventy-one naval ships were built, the most famous being the *Agamemnon* which was launched in 1781. The Agamemnon was Nelson's first command and his favourite ship.

An extensive network of long-distance walks has many of its routes in Hampshire. The South Downs Way starts at Winchester and continues eastward for 106 miles to Eastbourne. The Solent Way follows the Hampshire coastline eastward for 60 miles from Milford-on-Sea to Emsworth. The Test Way is a beautiful 50-mile valley walk from Totton northwards to Inkpen Beacon. For the enthusiast, a round trip of 160 miles can be achieved by linking the Test Way, the Wayfarer's Walk and the Solent Way.

The largest wild area in lowland Britain is the New Forest, established by William the Conqueror in 1079 as a royal hunting preserve. At that time oak, beech and birch were conspicuous by their absence; the 500 square miles of 'forest' consisted mainly of open heath and grassland. To protect his hunting, the King imposed a strict 'Forest Law' on the commoners. Bows and arrows, deer traps, hunting at night and enclosing their own land were all outlawed. Their only compensation was the right to graze livestock freely anywhere in the forest.

By the later Middle Ages there was a growing demand for timber, both for building and for ships. The *Inclosure Act* of 1482 banished all animals from parts of the forest and allowed new areas of woodland to develop. In the quest for the preservation of the forest for timber, the use of it as a hunting ground diminished; by the 17th century it had ceased altogether.

In the early 13th century the dreaded Forest Law was replaced with the more understanding Court of the Verderers (Verderer is from the Norman 'vert' – the 'green' of the woodland). Today this same court still administers some commoners' rights: to collect firewood; to graze livestock freely and the right of 'Pannage' – to allow pigs to forage in the autumn woods for acorns and beech mast. To chance upon a herd of pigs wandering at will around the woods and lanes of the forest is one of its unexpected delights.

The New Forest was again put to practical use during both World Wars: timber was taken, ammunition stored and the undulating terrain used as a training ground. Today, at only 145 square miles, the forest's main adversary is the motor car. Once that is left behind, there is a wonderland to explore: magnificent woods, quiet sylvan glades where streams trickle through, and wild, open moorland. The forest is a constant delight in any season. In autumn it has a glory all its own: if you miss the autumn colour, don't despair – to walk among the myriad dry crackling leaves in early winter, as gentle sunlight filters through the leafless trees, is a special joy reserved only for walkers – young and old alike!

Tea Shops

Whether a walk is taken as a gentle stroll or a good brisk hike, what better way to end it than with a good pot of tea and a home-made scone (preferably warm) with rich, fresh (calorie-raising – but the walk's taken care of that) clotted cream.

The routes are arranged so that a tea shop comes at, or near the end of, each walk; some even have a further choice *en route*. We have, where there has been a choice of tea shops, chosen the one we think most suits the rambler's needs i.e. usually those with a garden so that rucksacks don't get in the way and the summer sun can be enjoyed. You may therefore find yourself enjoying tea and scones in the flower-filled garden of a pretty thatched cottage, feeding the ducks from a riverside tea shop or sitting outside a seafront café, where a fresh sea breeze always seems to enhance the taste buds. The tea shops offer a good variety of home-made cakes and scones: all, except one, serve lunches – some a full roast, others perhaps just soup (usually home-made) and sandwiches. One or two even serve an early breakfast! They all welcome ramblers, muddy boots excepted of course. Most will appreciate advance notice of the arrival of a walking group. As the majority are individually owned, opening hours can be a little erratic, especially in winter – a season which in itself varies from tea shop to tea shop. Therefore a telephone call before persuading the family to leave the fireside on a cold winter's day could perhaps save a lot of disappointment!

The Walks

The twenty-six circular walks range from 4 to 8½ miles and are suitable for anyone of reasonable fitness.

The walks have been graded and range from an easy stroll around Jane Austen's beloved Chawton to the very strenuous Petersfield ramble (rewarded by the views which so inspired the poet Edward Thomas). Between these two extremes the walks explore the beautiful valleys and villages of the Rivers Test, Meon and Avon; the ancient woods and undulating moorland of the New Forest; the Hampshire Basin and the historic towns of Romsey and Winchester.

Good, stout shoes, preferably walking boots, are recommended, especially when walking on chalk downland and forest paths, which can be very slippery. Carrying wet weather gear is a sensible precaution and, even on a tea shop walk, a flask containing a hot drink adds enjoyment to all but the shortest of walks.

The maps referred to are the Ordnance Survey (OS) Landranger series 1:50 000 (1¼ inches to 1 mile) and Pathfinder, Outdoor Leisure and Explorer series 1:25 000 (2½ inches to 1 mile). All the footpaths are on Public Rights of Way or Permissive Paths (paths where the owner permits public use). Sketch maps are numbered to correspond with the text and should be sufficient for most of the walks: however, as the forest paths are not always well defined, an OS map and a compass is advisable when walking in the New Forest. OS maps provide a more detailed description of the surrounding area, identify features not mentioned in the text and generally add more interest and enjoyment to the walks. An OS grid reference is given to locate the start of each walk.

The walks have been checked but stiles and gates can fall into disrepair and footpaths are occasionally re-routed. Please inform your local Ramblers Association Group if you meet any obstructions or diversions.

Additional information is included on interesting places and features passed on the walks. We hope you enjoy discovering some of the county's ancient history, its wildlife and more than a little of its natural beauty – happy walking!

Public Transport

Where possible the names of public transport operators have been given. For further information contact the operator referred to at the beginning of each walk.

Bus services

Stagecoach Hampshire Bus	01256 464 501
Stagecoach Coastline Buses	01705 498 894
Solent Blue Line	01703 226 235
Provincial Buses	01329 232 208
Wilts & Dorset	01202 673 555
Skylark Motor Service	01725 510 282
Oakley Coaches	01256 780 731
Broughton & Mottisfont Village Bus	01794 301 458
Hants & Sussex Motor Service	01243 372 025

Train services

Mid-Hants Railway	01962 733 810
All other train inquiries	0345 484 950

1. Winchester & St Catherine's Hill

Route: Once the 112 steps at the beginning of this walk have been conquered and the superb view enjoyed, the route follows the River Itchen through lush meadows into Winchester. This is a beautiful walk for any season. Allow plenty of time though, as it would be a shame not to visit the Hospital of St Cross or St Swithun's Church. If you haven't visited it in the past, time should be allowed to absorb the breathtaking beauty of Winchester Cathedral.

Tea shop: On our walk we 'took refuge' in the **Cathedral Refectory**. Snacks, hot meals, cream teas and home-made cakes were served by friendly, volunteer helpers. The refectory is large, with extra seating in a walled courtyard – but it is very popular! If you find it just too busy, there is an abundance of tea shops in the town. The Refectory is open daily from 9.30am-5.00pm (April-October) and 9.30am-4.30pm (November-March). It is closed on Good Friday, Christmas Day and New Year. Tel: 01962 853 224.

Distance: 4½ miles.

How to get there: Leave the city centre via Southgate Street (B3335). After ¾ mile turn left into Kingsgate Road then right along Garnier Road for ¼ mile to the car park on the right.

Public Transport: Bus services: Stagecoach Hampshire Bus, Solent Blue Line. Trains: South West Trains.

Start: GR 484280. St Catherine's Hill car park (free).

Maps: Landranger 185; Explorer 132; Pathfinder 1264 SU41/51.

1. Leave the car park via the railway bridge in the far corner. Pass through a kissing-gate and ascend to a further kissing-gate. From the gate, the path climbs to the left, levels out for a short distance then turns right and ascends, via a flight of 112 steps, to the summit of St Catherine's Hill and the mizmaze.

    The view here is breathtaking. Trees, of all shades of green, stretch as far as the eye can see. Standing proud above the canopy are the towers of Winchester Cathedral and the Hospital of St Cross. Below, the ribbon-

like River Itchen snakes its way through the valley. In their seasons, the hill is carpeted with an amazing variety of beautiful chalk-loving wild flowers.

St Catherine's Hill was once the site of an Iron Age fort; its ditch and ramparts can still be seen. From the 12th to the 16th century there was a Norman Chapel here dedicated to St Catherine; all that remains today is a mound in the beech trees. The turf mizmaze is one of only eight such mazes in the country; its origin is unknown. There are two schools of thought: that monks traversed them on their knees as an act of penance; or they were provided for fun at fairs.

2. From the mizmaze turn right to the city viewpoint. When you've taken your fill of the superb view, turn left and walk halfway round the hill, gradually descending to a gravel path: a wooden pole on the path indicates steps down. Descend via the steps then pass through two gates to the river. Turn left onto a pleasant tree-lined path alongside the riverbank. Turn left to pass under a disused railway bridge and continue on a road.

3. Turn first right towards St Cross. The road crosses a series of bridges to which it owes its name 'Five Bridges Road' and a lovely stretch of the River Itchen. Just beyond the fifth bridge turn right along a farm track. Cross two stiles, thoughtfully placed to keep walkers away from a muddy section, then keep ahead, following a stream on your left. Cross a stile and footbridge and pass through an avenue of lime trees. Soon the Hospital of St Cross comes into view.

The Hospital of St Cross is Britain's oldest charitable institution. Henry de Blois, Bishop of Winchester and grandson of William the Conqueror, founded it in 1136, at a time of great hardship. Accommodation was provided for thirteen sick and needy men; a daily meal given to one hundred poor men and bread and wine, 'The Wayfarer's Dole', to all weary travellers who knocked at its doors. The chapel was built some thirty years later; it has a beautiful, interesting interior. In the north transept there is a unique 'Bird-Beak' window — to explain it would spoil the surprise. In the 15th century, Cardinal Beaufort added the elegant, tall chimneyed Almshouse of Noble Poverty. Today, in this idyllic setting, where vast lawns sweep down to the river and swans glide gracefully by, these beautiful buildings exude an aura of peace and tranquillity. Accommodation is provided for 25 Brothers and the Wayfarer's Dole (now a token only) is still given to all who care to enter. The hospital is open to visitors Monday to Saturday; summer until 5pm; winter until 3.30pm. For further information tel: 01962 851 375.

Interestingly, Anthony Trollope's novel, *The Warden*, is based on the history of St Cross and it's of little surprise to learn that these beautiful meadows and the riverside walk inspired John Keats to write his ode 'To Autumn' during a stay in Winchester in 1819.

'The Almshouse of Noble Poverty'

4. Where the hospital wall turns left, keep ahead across the field to a footbridge. Continue alongside a stream, passing a footbridge to Waterhead Road, until reaching a further road. Cross over to walk between the grounds of Winchester College and the Itchen.

Winchester College was founded in 1382 by William of Wykeham. His architect was the brilliant William Wynford, who was later responsible, with Wykeham, for the magnificent cathedral nave. The college, conceived as a school for 70 poor scholars and 10 fee paying 'commoners', is the oldest

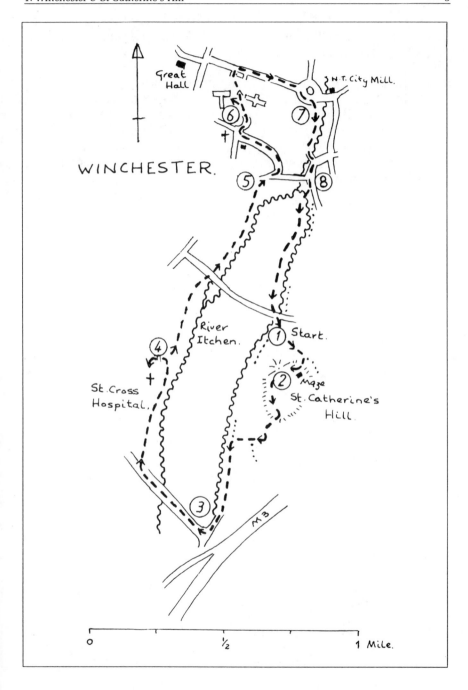

school in England. Wykeham gave the college the famous motto, 'Manners Makyth Man'.

5. On reaching a parking area, turn right to the road. Turn left along College Walk, then left again into College Street. At the end of the college buildings is the house in which Jane Austen spent her last days. Turn right and pass through Kingsgate; with the charming medieval church of St Swithun atop. Kingsgate is one of five gates mentioned in the city's ancient history. Turn right into the cathedral grounds.

Winchester Cathedral, one of the most beautiful buildings in the county, is a glorious monument to centuries of ancient history and superb craftsmanship. It is the burial place of bishops and pre-Conquest kings; where Mary Tudor was married to the King of Spain and where Izaak Walton and Hampshire's Jane Austen are buried. To attempt to describe its glory here, would be to do it a grave injustice: no matter how many times it is visited, there will always be something to marvel and wonder at. The cathedral was founded by King Alfred's son, Edward the Elder. Work started in 1079 and it was consecrated in 1093. Timber for the cathedral roof came from nearby Hampage Wood. It is said that William the Conqueror had allowed Bishop Walkelyn, the first Norman Bishop, to take as many trees as he could in three days. The Bishop employed an army of men who worked night and day and stripped the wood of every tree, except one. William was not amused but the cathedral got its splendid roof. The most important alteration to the fabric of the cathedral occurred in the 14th century when William of Wykeham, the bishop to whom we owe so much, remodelled the nave to give the awe-inspiring magnificence we see today. In 1905, it was discovered that the building was sinking. We owe the cathedral's continued existence to the skill of William Walker, an experienced diver, who spent five years working under the building, removing boggy peat and underpinning it with scaffolding, bags of cement and concrete blocks. Conditions were so bad that artificial light could not be put in and Walker worked by torch alone. There is a statue of William Walker in the cathedral; he is wearing a diving suit.

6. Leave the Cathedral grounds by the diagonal path across the green. Pass through 'The Square' and turn right along High Street. (Turn left on leaving The Square if you wish to visit the

Great Hall, the only remains of Henry III's castle and home of the famous Arthurian Round Table). Continue along Broadway, passing the Guildhall, the Visitors' Centre (with a tea room), the Abbey Gardens – founded by King Alfred's wife, Queen Ealswith, and King Alfred's statue.

King Alfred's imposing bronze statue justifiably dominates the main thoroughfare. At the time of Alfred's coronation in 871, battles had been raging against the Danes for over ten years; the city was exhausted and in despair. In 878, the Danes drove Alfred back to a refuge in.Somerset. Here he took stock, gathered together his troops and made a surprise attack. A decisive victory was achieved: Alfred and King Guthrum settled peace terms and by 880, the Danes had left Wessex.

To guard against further invasions Alfred reorganised the city's defences and built ships twice as large and fast as the long boats of the Vikings. At heart a man of peace, he next turned his genius to more domestic matters. He laid out a network of modern street patterns, which made him the first English Town Planner; he encouraged law and good government and carried out a programme of education which was to make Winchester the home of all learning. Alfred was the first king to write in English; he was responsible for, and contributed to, the 'Anglo--Saxon Chronicle' one of the most comprehensive histories of the world. Alfred died in 899; his remains are believed to be in the vicinity of Hyde Abbey at the northern end of the city.

7. On reaching the City Mill on the bridge, turn right along Riverside Walk. (The 1744 mill, rebuilt by the National Trust in 1973, is the only mill in Winchester to survive relatively unaltered). Within a few metres pass the last visible remains of the City's Roman Walls. Where the path divides, keep left alongside the river. Behind the wall on the right lie the ruins of Wolvesley Castle, the main residence of the Bishops of Winchester throughout the Middle Ages. Leave the river over the bridge in front of the converted Wharf Mill.

8. Turn right along Wharf Hill. As the road sweeps right, cross over into a road signposted 'Private Road No Parking'. After 40 metres turn right and follow the Itchen Way through lush green meadows back to the car park.

2. New Alresford

Route: Undulating fields with panoramic views; ascending farm tracks
                        bordered by hedgerows, laden in their seasons with an abundance of
                        chalk-loving wild flowers; and two delightful strolls along the clear
                        waters of the River Alre. Alresford is a picture in summertime when the
                        main streets are aglow with colourful hanging flower baskets.

Tea shop: **Café Cresson** in Broad Street serves a good range of home-made
                        cakes, scones and lunches. There is extra seating in an attractive
                        garden patio. It is open Tuesday-Sunday, 10.00am-5.30pm.
                        Tel: 01962 733246.

Distance: 6 miles.

How to get there: Alresford is on the A31, 7 miles east of Winchester.

Public Transport: Bus service: Stagecoach Hampshire Bus. Trains: Mid-Hants
                        Watercress Line – Hampshire's Steam Railway.

Start: GR 588325. Alresford Railway Station car park (free Sundays & Bank
                        Holidays).

Maps: Landranger 185; Explorer 132; Pathfinder 1243 SU43/53.

From 1865, Alresford was a station on the Alton to Winchester railway line. Despite strong campaigning by local residents, including the late John Arlott, the cricket commentator, the line closed in 1973. Four years later a ten mile stretch of the line was re-opened by a local preservation society as 'The Watercress Line', a nickname given to the original line by watercress growers, its main users, when transporting their cress to London. The Watercress Line runs through scenic countryside between Alresford and Alton, with two stations *en route*; all the stations have original fittings. Huge powerful locomotives bellowing forth clouds of smoke, draw crowds of steam enthusiasts, some even accompanied by their children, to the station at weekends and Bank Holidays.

1. From the car park walk down Station Road as far as the public toilets. Turn left along a passage between houses. At the road, turn right, reach West Street junction and cross into The Dean.

The Watercress Line

At the end of The Dean turn left for a pleasant walk along the River Alre. Shortly pass the grave of an Alsatian mascot of the US 47th infantry. Cross a footbridge by an ancient mill race and soon another footbridge. Ignore an ascending path on the right and continue ahead. Reach the road and keep ahead for 30 metres.

The Wayfarer's Walk is a 70-mile scenic route from Emsworth in Hampshire, along the Solent coast, through the Meon Valley and Watership Down to Inkpen Beacon in Berkshire.

2. Turn right onto the Wayfarer's Walk (WW). Steadily ascend for some 450 metres, then descend for a similar distance to a T-junction. Turn left, cross a stream and continue on a track, passing watercress beds on the right.

3. Soon pass a cottage on the right and steadily climb for ½ mile to a road. Here, leave the Wayfarer's Walk and turn right downhill. At a junction, turn right towards Alresford. At the next junction, turn left and rejoin the Wayfarer's Walk; the lane soon degenerates into rough gravel. Turn right along a bridleway (WW) between large open fields.

4. On passing a large barn on the left, turn right towards Alresford and climb alongside a right-hand field boundary. At the top of the field, cross a stile into another field. Follow a line of cables across this field: pause at the summit to enjoy the marvellous 360-degree view of the surrounding countryside.

5. Pass a long, semi-circular metal barn on the left and the following three electricity poles. Just before the fourth pole, turn right through a gap in a hedge. Follow a left-hand field boundary for 250 metres to a stile in the hedgerow. Cross the stile and bear slightly right across a field. At the far side of the field turn right along the boundary, walking at the rear of houses.

6. Turn left for 10 metres then right onto a driveway: although marked 'private road' this is a right of way. Pass Manor Farm Barns then a detached house. Sixty metres beyond the house turn right over a stile and follow a left-hand hedgerow across two fields. Depending on the season, you may see the watercress

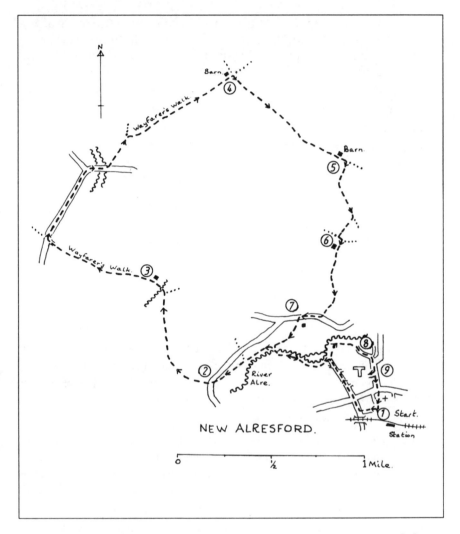

NEW ALRESFORD.

beds on the far side of the hedge. Continue along a gravel drive-way to a road. Turn right.

7. Immediately beyond Pinglestone Farm, turn left over a stile. Within a few metres turn right over a further stile. A sign here requests that an alternative route is used; we stayed with the right of way – you may decide otherwise. Bear left across the field to a stile at the end of a conifer plantation. Skirt the plantation to a

stile on the left. From the stile turn left to retrace the route along the riverbank. Reach The Dean and turn left along the riverbank, shortly pass a picturesque timber and thatch cottage 'Fulling Mill' straddling the river; and the Memorial Gardens.

Fulling was a process which closed together the woven threads of material to shrink and tighten it. Waterpower was used to drive the hammers which kneaded and pressed the cloth. A mill existed here in the 13th century; for several hundred years the air resounded to the hammering of the fulling stocks. The Fulling Mill, now a delightful cottage in an idyllic setting, was renovated in 1951 by a private buyer.

8. Follow a quiet country lane to a junction. Turn right and immediately pass a beautiful half-timbered cottage, 'Timbers' with an ancient sundial high on its wall. Continue along Broad Street to the tea shop.

Alresford is built around three main streets which form the letter 'T'. Its focal point is the lovely, tree-lined Broad Street, which since the 1200s has been the town's market place. From medieval times the town prospered from its wool trade: sheep fairs held here survived into the 20th century. Over the centuries, Alresford suffered devastating fires. After the last dreadful fire in 1736, it was ordered that instead of thatch, wattle and daub, the town be rebuilt in brick and tile. Today we have a charming Georgian town, with many of its houses and cottages imaginatively painted in attractive pastel shades.

Alresford residents have always benefited from watercress growing wild in the clear, free-flowing, chalk stream-beds; but it was too perishable to be transported along the poor country roads to other markets. The coming of the railway put London hotels and markets within reach: the industry and Arlesford prospered. Today, locally grown cress is available throughout the town in bunches, soups, sandwiches and even pancakes.

9. From the tea shop, turn right to the end of Broad Street. Cross to Barclays Bank and take the path to the parish church. Walk through the grounds keeping the church on your left. Turn right along a passage, then left to return to the car park.

3. Chawton & Upper Farringdon

Route: An easy, almost level walk, through landscape beloved by Jane
                    Austen. Thatched cottages, ancient woodland, fields and hedgerows
                    flourishing with wild flowers, epitomize the beauty of Hampshire's
                    countryside. With Jane's lovely home to visit at the end, this is the ideal
                    walk for a lazy, summer's day.

Tea shop: Opposite Jane Austen's house is **Cassandra's Cup**. Crisp table linen,
                    matching china, an excellent range of home-made cakes and lunches,
                    plus a tiny 'Aladdin's cave' gift shop, guarantee an enjoyable visit.
                    There is seating outside. Open: April to October, 10.30am-4.30pm,
                    Tuesday-Sunday. November and December, Thursday-Sunday. In
                    January and February, weekends only; and in March,
                    Wednesday-Sunday. Tel: 01420 83144.

Distance: 5 miles.

How to get there: Chawton is one mile south-west of Alton. It is signposted off the
                    roundabout at the junction of the A31 Winchester road with the A32
                    Fareham road.

Public Transport: Bus service: Provincial Buses.

Start: GR 709375. Village car park (free) opposite Jane Austen's house.

Maps: Landranger 186; Explorer 133; Pathfinder 1244. SW63/73

---

1. Return to the road and turn sharp left by the telephone box. Pass
    a terrace of pretty thatched cottages and shortly the parish
    church, the burial place of Jane Austen's mother and sister, Cas-
    sandra. At the end of the lane, a narrow path leads up to the main
    road. Here turn left: the road is very busy so keep well in to the
    grass verge. In approximately $\frac{1}{4}$ mile turn left over a stile into a
    field. Cross diagonally right to a wide gateway. Through the gate,
    gently ascend between fields to a wood. The track initially as-
    cends through the wood; levels out along an avenue of stately
    Scots pine, then descends between yew to Upper Farringdon.
    Continue ahead alongside a children's playground then turn left
    along a narrow footpath. Turn right then left into Church Road.

Farringdon is an unusual village: it has pretty 16th century thatched cottages, a welcoming country inn, an ancient church – and its very own folly!

The parish church dates from the 12th century; however, two ancient yews guarding the church path suggest that the site may have been a place of pre-Christian worship. Gilbert White (see walk 4) was curate here from 1761 to 1785, riding over from his home in Selborne. An excellent church leaflet also relates a brief history of Farringdon.

In Church Road is the remarkable red-brick building known as Massey's Folly. Designed and built by Thomas Hackett Massey, a rector from 1857-1919, and helped only by three tradesmen, it took thirty years to complete. The building stood empty for the next fifteen years, until, in 1925, it was put to use as the village hall and school. The design is said to have been influenced by a recluse, the daughter of an Indian civil servant, who visited the rectory by means of a secret passage.

2. **From Church Road turn right into Crows Lane. At the Rose & Crown public house turn left along a narrow footpath. Enter a field and turn immediately left. Follow the boundary round to a stile on your left. Over the stile continue with the boundary on your right across two fields. Turn right over a double stile and cross a field to the farmhouse ahead. Turn left onto the farm track. On reaching a lane, turn right: this quiet country lane twists and turns for ¼ mile to a wide track on the left.**

3. **Turn left through a barrier gate and follow the track past a lovely young plantation of larch, beech, oak, alder and lime. As the track turns left, turn sharp right between a small plantation right and a mature hedgerow left. Pass through a metal gate into a field. Follow the line of Caker Stream across three fields via a footbridge, a horse jump, then a further footbridge to a stile at the end of the third field. Over the stile turn immediately left to go through a wooden gate into a conservation area.**

The area is being redesigned over a period of ten years. Hedges are being planted and laid, ponds restored and arable fields sown with chalkland and grassland flowers. When completed, this tiny haven will show how delightful the meadows were when Jane Austen and her sister walked through them to visit their young friends at the rectory in Farringdon.

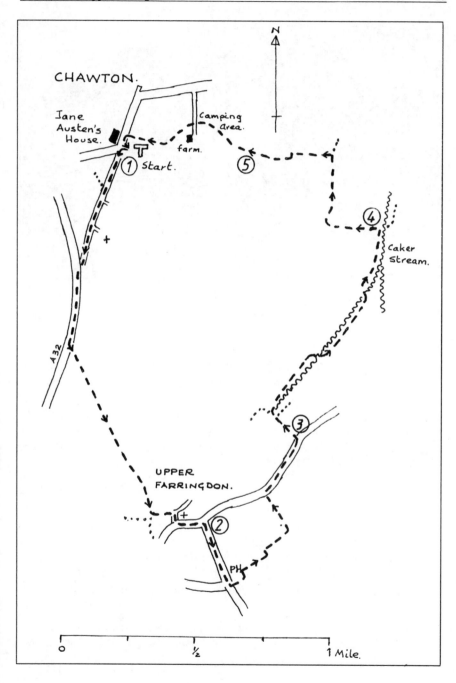

Jane Austen's house

4. A waymarked grassy path leads through the area to a well-placed seat and ornamental tree, then turns right towards a farmhouse. Shortly before reaching the farmhouse, leave the conservation area via a gate and turn immediately left through a further gate into a field. Continue ahead alongside a right-hand hedgerow. At the end of the field, pass through a metal gate then bear diagonally right to a double stile.

5. Over the stile follow waymarks across four small fields, heading towards a farmhouse and keeping to the right of the farm buildings. Cross the farm track to a stile, then bear left to a stile in the corner of the field. From the stile, descend a narrow path. Cross a stile and bear left to cross a further stile. Go straight across a field to a stile in a brick wall, from which a narrow path leads to the main road. Turn left to Jane Austen's House, the teashop and car park.

Hampshire is justly proud of its famous literary daughter, Jane Austen. Born in the village of Steventon in 1775, Jane moved to Chawton with her mother and sister, Cassandra, in 1809. Here, in a simple 17th century house, she spent the last eight years of her short life. After some years of unsettlement, the peace and happiness she enjoyed in her new surroundings provided the inspiration to resume her writings. *Sense and Sensibility* and *Pride and Prejudice* were revised and published in 1811 and 1813. *Mansfield Park, Emma* and *Persuasion* followed in quick succession. Sadly, during the writing of her last, and unfinished novel, *Sanditon*, Jane became ill with a tubercular disease. In 1817 she moved, with Cassandra, to Winchester for specialist treatment. Unfortunately, at that time, there was no cure and Jane died in her sister's arms on 18 July 1817. She is buried in Winchester Cathedral.

Jane's home is now a lovingly restored private museum. An extensive collection of personal and family mementos includes letters written by Jane herself. For further information, tel: 01420 83262.

4. Selborne Hanger

Route: A pleasant country walk through open meadows and mixed woodland. The paths undulate throughout, with two short woodland climbs. There are lovely views at many stages. The circuit ends with the descent of Gilbert White's famous zigzag path.

Tea shop: Sixteenth century **Bush House** is a very traditional oak-beamed restaurant and tea room. Excellent home-made meals and delightful cakes and scones are served on matching crockery – with a proper, capacious teapot! There is a large attractive garden with a sun-trap patio. It is open daily in summer: 10.30am-5.00pm; winter until 4.00pm, but closed Tuesdays and all January. Tel: 01420 511 339.

Distance: 5½ miles.

How to get there: Selborne is on the B3006 between Alton and Petersfield.

Public Transport: Bus services: Stagecoach Hampshire Bus, Provincial Buses.

Start: GR 742335. Selborne car park (free).

Maps: Landranger 186; Explorer 133; Pathfinder 1244 SU63/73.

Picturesque Selborne shelters under the steep beech-clad slopes of Selborne Hanger. The village is famous for being the home of the 18th century naturalist and author, Reverend Gilbert White. His love for Selborne and the beautiful surrounding countryside was so great, that rather than be a vicar elsewhere, he chose to remain a curate in Hampshire, first at Farringdon (see walk 3) and later in Selborne. The Reverend's great joy was in his daily observations of all that happened, in nature, around him; nothing was too minute or trivial to be recorded in his diaries. However, his greatest interest was the study of birds and their daily life. His celebrated book *A Natural History of Selborne* gives a vivid, fascinating and detailed account of wildlife in and around Selborne; it makes delightful reading. In St Mary's church, built around 1180, and little changed, there is a first edition of *The Natural History*. One of two magnificent windows commemorating his life depicts Selborne, all the birds mentioned in his book and St Francis of Assisi. Gilbert White is buried on the north side of the church; his stone is marked with the simple

'The Wakes'

inscription G.W. 26th June 1793. Sadly the church's famous 1400-year-old yew was blown over in the January 1990 storms; all that re-mains is a sad-looking stump.

'The Wakes', Gilbert White's home, is now a museum. It com-memorates not only the life of Gilbert White but also the Oates fam-ily. A fascinating exhibition on Captain Lawrence Oates includes relics of the ill-fated expedition to the South Pole.

1. Return to the road, turn left to walk through the village, passing **Bush House** *en route*. On reaching 'The Wakes', cross over to the green and follow the Hangers Way through the church grounds into Church Meadows. Keep to the Way as it takes you through the meadow and along both the Short and Long Lythes.

    The name 'Hanger' is derived from the Old English 'hangra' meaning wooded slope. The Hangers Way is a 21-mile walk, linking a series of hang-ers, from Alton to Petersfield (walk 5) and beyond to Queen Elizabeth Country Park (walk 6). It passes through some of the most beautiful and varied countryside in Hampshire. The word 'lythe' is thought to be Anglo-Saxon and possibly meant a woodland path. Wild flowers early in the year include primroses, sweet violet and wood sorrel. Later, dog rose, wood spurge and common helebore catch the eye.

2. At the end of Long Lythe, a kissing-gate leads into a meadow. Continue along the top of the meadow until reaching a wooden gate at the corner of the wood. Here, bear right to a footbridge and stile. Over the stile, head uphill to a waymarker at the corner of the woodland. Turn right to reach a stile. Over the stile follow a broad woodland path for 75 metres to a stile on the left, at the top of the bank.

3. From the stile, bear right through the wood, keeping parallel to the fence on the right. Cross a stile into a field. Continue ahead for 5 metres, then turn left across the field. Keep to the left of an electricity pole in the middle of the field. At the end of the field cross a stile and turn left along a wide track. The track dips and rises as it meanders through Wick Wood. On leaving the wood maintain the same direction, alongside a field on your right, until reaching a wooden, padlocked gate into the field.

4. Twenty-five metres beyond the gate, turn acute left to ascend Wick Hill Hanger. Leave the hanger via a stile into a field. In the distance on the left, Selborne Hanger can be seen. Continue directly ahead towards a farmhouse. Pass through a gate and turn right along a lane. As the lane sweeps right, take a wide gravel track on the left. Within a few metres pass Wick Hill Cottages and continue along the now grassy path between woodland and fields. The path eventually leaves the woods and turns right across open fields. As you gradually descend across the fields, Selborne Hanger can again be seen over to the left: if you stop and look carefully you should be able to see the zigzag through the trees.

5. On reaching the road, cross directly over into a large field. Follow the right-hand boundary until reaching a footbridge. Over the footbridge, head across the field towards two stiles. Cross the stile on the left and turn sharp right up the field. Cross a stile and keep ahead, between trees, to a field. Follow the right-hand boundary down to a gate. Pass through the gate to a lane and keep

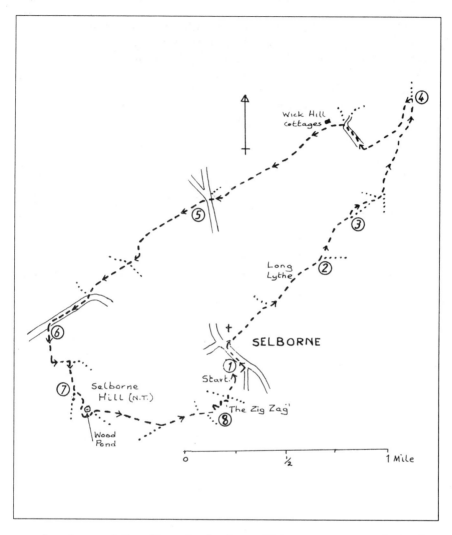

ahead round the elbow in the lane. This quiet country lane, between fields, soon reaches a wood on the left.

6. Turn left over a stile to skirt the wood. Just before reaching a field
    turn left onto a waymarked footpath. In 15 metres, pass through a
    wooden gate and follow the top edge of the field to a stile on the
    right. Cross the stile into Selborne Common and turn right to as-
    cend Selborne Hill.

7. On reaching a permissive horse route notice, fork left onto the bridleway. At the first junction (there is a bridleway post 15 metres ahead) turn right for 65 metres to a small pond on the left. Walk round the pond to the seat on the far side. From the seat follow a path which leads, at a right angle, directly away from the pond across the heathland. At a junction, turn left onto the main path through Selborne Hanger.

Gilbert White described the hanger as 'a vast hill of chalk, rising three hundred feet above the village; and is divided into a sheep-down, the high wood, and a long hanging wood called a hanger. The cover of this eminence is altogether beech, the most lovely of all forest trees.' The zigzag path was built with the help of his brother in 1753: the wishing stone at the summit is sarsen stone.

8. Continue through the hanger until reaching a metal seat near the wishing stone and the zigzag. Descend the zigzag, pass through a gate and follow the footpath back to the car park and the village.

5. Petersfield and Ashford Hanger

Route: This strenuous ramble includes a long steep climb up Lythe Hanger
                   and a short, steep descent from Ashford Hanger: the chalk tracks are
                   slippery after rain. There is an excellent pub for a lunch stop and
                   magnificent views from the top of Ashford Hanger. The best time is
                   perhaps early spring when daffodils and wild primroses are out and
                   foliage free trees allow expansive views.

Tea shop: **The Folly Tree Coffee Shop** is adjacent to Folly Market. Its
                   wide-ranging menu offers breakfast, lunches and cream teas. There is
                   an attractive courtyard. Open summer: Monday-Saturday,
                   8.00am-6.00pm, Sunday, 10.00am-5.00pm. Winter; Monday-Saturday
                   8.00am-5.00pm, Sunday 10.00am-4.00pm. Tel: 01730 267 432.

Distance: 7½ miles.

How to get there: Petersfield is signposted off the A3(T), 17 miles north of Portsmouth.

Public Transport: Bus services: Stagecoach Coastline Buses, Stagecoach Hampshire
                   Bus, Solent Blue Line, Provincial Buses. Trains: South West Trains.

Start: GR 743235. Petersfield Railway Station car park(free weekends and
                   Bank Holidays).

Maps: Landranger 197; Explorer 133; Pathfinder 1265 (SU 62/72).

Petersfield has been a market town since the 12th century. The town
prospered as a wool market in the 14th century, when buyers from
the continent came to purchase high quality Downland wool. In the
19th century it was a main stopping place on the London to Portsmouth road; eleven inns provided hospitality for up to thirty passenger coaches a day. Today, Petersfield is a pleasant mixture of
Georgian, Victorian and modern buildings. At the top of the High
Street is a half-timbered building rebuilt in 1997 after a devastating
fire. In the large Town Square there is an unusual equestrian statue
of William III. Resplendent in Roman robes, with a laurel wreath on
his head, the King sits astride an immense horse with a bow on its
tail. He deserved better: it was King William who introduced the Bill
of Rights – the social contract between monarch and people, which
established Parliament as the supreme law-making body.

1. From the station, turn left over the level crossing. Walk down Station Road to the roundabout. Turn left towards Stroud then first right into Beckham Lane. At the last house in the lane turn right over a stile into a field. Diagonally cross two fields then go straight across a third field. Cross a stile and climb to the motorway footbridge.

2. Cross the bridge and turn left into a field. Continue parallel to the motorway until crossing a second stile, then turn right and cross the field to a stile. From the stile, cross three fields, via stiles and a footbridge, heading towards a large red-brick house on the right. Pass through a metal gate on the right of the house and turn left along a lane to a road. Cross over to a stile into a field. Bear right across two fields to a track. Cross the track and a stile into a field and cross diagonally to a double stile. Continue through a series of paddocks until reaching Lythe Farm.

3. Pass through the gateway of the house to a track on the left of the drive. The track climbs through Lythe Hanger. Initially the climb, between the fields, is almost imperceptible, but as the track turns left into the hanger, it becomes a steep, steady climb to the summit. At the summit is a private crossing, continue ahead for 40 metres to a junction. Turn left for 20 metres then turn right onto a lane and descend to Wheelers Farm on the right. At the end of the farm garden, turn right over a stile into a meadow. Cross diagonally left to a stile. Over the stile turn left into a field. Follow a right-hand boundary to a road. Turn right then left opposite High Croft Cottage.

4. Follow a right-hand field boundary to a stile to a lane. Turn left for 35 metres then turn right over a stile. Follow a left-hand field boundary down to a stile to a lane. Turn right along this quiet lane bordered by fields and light woodland. On reaching a sign for 'Pipers Farm', turn left over a stile into a field. Cross diagonally right, keeping to the left of a clump of five trees. At the bottom of the field keep to the left of a small copse in a hollow (a disused pit) and continue down to a stile. Cross a track to enter a field. Follow a left-hand boundary to a road. Cross diagonally right and continue along the drive of Rings Green Farm. Turn

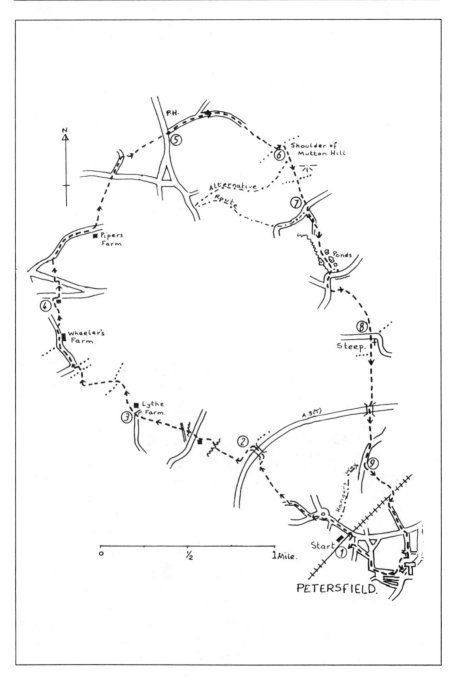

right through a gate into a field. Cross diagonally left, pass through a gate and continue along a footpath to a road.

5. If a break for refreshment is needed then turn left to the **Trooper Inn**. Otherwise cross the road into Honeycritch Lane. Where the lane turns left continue ahead along Old Litten Lane, which shortly becomes a tree-lined track. Reach a T-junction and turn left. After 50 metres, turn right along The Hangers Way to enter Ashford Hanger at the summit of The Shoulder of Mutton Hill.

Yes, the hill is said to represent that particular shape and that is its official name. The views from this steep chalk hillside are magnificent. Nestling in the valley below is Steep, with Petersfield beyond. On the horizon are the steep, wooded slopes of the South Downs.

6. Pass through a barrier to descend the hill. (The hill is exceptionally steep, you may prefer to turn right and follow an easier route down via The Hangers Way.)

Halfway down the hill is a monument to Edward Thomas, one of our great countryside writers, who lived in Steep for the last ten years of his life. A writer of books and prose, it was only in his last three years that he turned to poetry. It is this poetry, so simply and delightfully expressing his love and understanding of Hampshire's countryside, for which he is so popular today.

The hill is referred to in several of his poems. In 'Wind and Mist' the view inspired '... a hollow land as vast as heaven... Sixty miles of South Downs at one glance ...'. A quiet, private man,

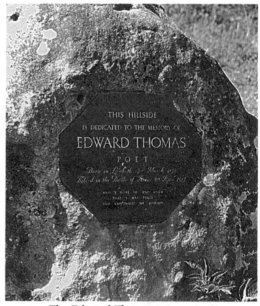

The Edward Thomas monument

Thomas was never to know how much his work is loved. He was killed on the first day of the Battle of Arras in 1917: he was 38. The hillside is dedicated to his memory. The sarsen memorial stone is inscribed, 'and I rose up and knew that I was tired and continued my journey.'

7. At the bottom of the hill continue across a field to a road. Turn right. After 20 metres turn left onto the Hangers Way. The path meanders through woodland then skirts it, with a woodland stream on the right. Immediately past a conservation area, 'Little Langley' turn right to cross a footbridge and descend to the road at Mill Corner. Turn right to a junction, then turn left through a kissing-gate into a field. Follow a right-hand hedgerow until reaching a stile. Over the stile, climb through woodland to Steep.

To emerge from the wood onto the large, wooded village green, with a beautiful 12th century church ahead, is the most delightful way to arrive at Steep. Inside the church, two small exquisitely beautiful windows, the work of Laurence Whistler, celebrate Edward Thomas. One window depicts the landscape so loved by Thomas; the other is engraved with one of his poems. A wonderful set of kneelers depicts the natural history of the area.

8. Follow the Hangers Way alongside the church, soon passing Bedales School on the right. Cross the footbridge over the motorway and follow a fenced footpath to a road. Continue ahead along the road.

9. On reaching a house, Tilmore Lea, leave the Hangers Way and turn left over a stile. (If you wish to go straight back to the station, cross over and continue along the Hangers Way). Follow a fenced path to a children's recreation ground. Cross the field, pass under a railway bridge and continue to a road. At the end of the road, cross into College Street. Turn right at the White Hart public house, follow the road round the pub to Folly Lane and the tea shop. Continue along the lane and turn right along High Street. Turn right along Chapel Street and left along Lavant Street to return to the station.

6. Buriton & Queen Elizabeth Country Park

Route: A strenuous but rewarding ramble, for the most part along ascending paths, with a steep climb to the summit of Windmill Hill. The woodland chalk slopes are very slippery after rain. The route passes through two picturesque villages; in their seasons there is an abundance of woodland wild flowers and the views from Windmill Hill are quite superb.

Tea shop: The **Coach House Café** is part of the Visitor Centre in Queen Elizabeth Country Park. The menu offers soup, sandwiches (hot bacon baguettes were the 'dish of the day' when we visited) and a good range of home-made cakes. There are picnic tables in a pleasant courtyard overlooking a wildlife pond. It is open daily, Easter-October, 10.00am-5.30pm. November-March, weekends only, 10.00am-5.30pm (or dusk). Tel:01705 596 345.

Distance: 8 miles.

How to get there: Buriton is east of the A3(T), 2 miles south of Petersfield.

Public Transport: Bus service: Provincial Buses.

Start: GR 740200. Buriton village pond, parking area in front of the church.

Maps: Landranger 197; Explorer 120; Pathfinder 1285 SU61/71.

A willow-fringed pond overlooked by a manor house and a 13th century ironstone church, sheltered in a peaceful valley protected by ancient woodland: a beautiful landscape which attracts walkers from near and far.

Buriton is also known for its association with two historic figures. One hundred years before Gilbert White (see walk 4), John Goodyer, the botanist, was appraising not only plants native to the area but also the first English potatoes – and tobacco. His reputation throughout England was so great that when the village was garrisoned during the Civil War, a protection order was put on his family, servants and all his estate. John Goodyer and his wife are buried in Buriton churchyard.

Buriton village pond

The manor house was the boyhood home of Edward Gibbon, author of the famous *History of the Decline and Fall of the Roman Empire*. Gibbon loved the quiet of the village and its beauty. He described the aspect as 'various and cheerful: the downs commanded a noble prospect; and the long hanging wood in sight of the house could not perhaps have been improved by art or expense.'

1. With the church on your left, cross to a stile into Buriton Estates and ascend the field to a stile into a wood. The chalk track climbs steeply to a summit then levels out and meanders through to a lane.

2. Turn right for 55 metres then left over a stile for a long gradual climb through woodland. (In late spring there is an amazing show of cowslips and orchids here.) Continue ahead when the path merges with a wide, grassy path from the right. This pleasant level path leads through Head Down Plantation, a fine beech plantation, then descends through Head Down Hanger to a wide crossing track.

3. Cross the track and follow a short, narrow path to a stile into a large, arable field. Cross the field, keeping to the right of a pylon ahead then left of the next one, to reach a stile. Turn left along a lane. On reaching a track to the old level crossing, turn right onto a byway and climb steadily to a summit with far reaching views. Note the windmill high on Windmill Hill and look back at the beautiful view north east to West Harting Down and northwest to the Country Park. Reach a road and turn right to descend to Chalton. At the green, turn left to the parish church and the public house.

Nestling on the western slopes of Chalton Down, with a picture-postcard view of the windmill high on the hill, Chalton is a small attractive village, much smaller today than in the Middle Ages, when St Michael's was the mother church for a wide area. The early Norman church has a spacious, pleasing interior. The Red Lion is one of the best examples of a wealden house in Hampshire and is reputed to be its oldest inn. According to local legend it was once a workshop for tradesmen who rebuilt the church.

4. Turn right along the Petersfield road for almost ½ mile. Just after going under electricity cables turn left over a stile. Cross a field diagonally right. In a second field, keep left of a lone dead tree and climb steeply to the top of the field – not quite at the summit yet, but pause for a breather and to admire the fantastic views. Bear right and reach a stile on the left, up three steps, then follow a fenced path to a lane. Turn left to reach the summit of Windmill Hill and the windmill.

The earliest reference to a windmill at Chalton is dated 1289. This mill, dated 1785, was rescued from dereliction in 1980 and rebuilt as a private house. The amazing views are east along the ridge of the Downs and south to Chichester Harbour and the Isle of Wight.

5. Turn back along the lane. Immediately after it curves right, turn right over a stile in the hedgerow. Bear left over the brow of a field and maintain the same direction across a second field to a stile in the hedgerow.

Butser Ancient Farm, seen on the right, is a reconstructed Iron Age farm settlement. The wattle and daub roundhouses are very evocative, especially on a cold, quiet winter's day. Using replica Iron Age tools, the

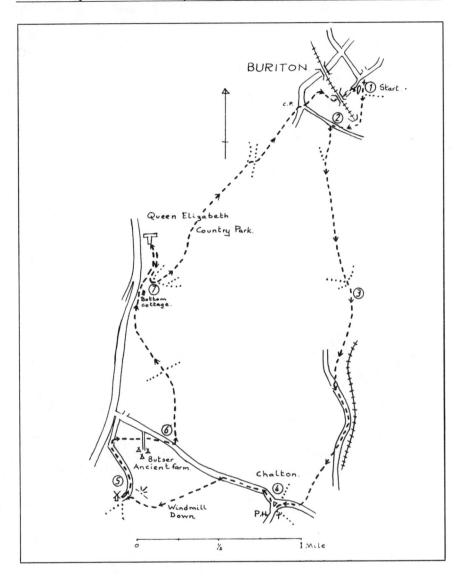

farm is recreating agricultural processes of some 2,000 years ago. Visitors are encouraged to try their hands at spinning, weaving, grinding corn and feeding the livestock.

For further information, tel: 01705 598 838.

6. Cross the road diagonally right to a track which rises and falls through the valley and skirts the Country Park. Pass Bottom Cottage (see note) and turn right into the park. Cross a picnic area to a main driveway. Cross the drive diagonally right, pass through a gateway and continue to the Visitor Centre and the café.

Bottom Cottage was once an inn on the London to Portsmouth road. It was featured in Charles Dickens' Nicholas Nickleby when Nicholas and Smike 'sallied forth to seek their fortunes.'

The Country Park comprises 1,400 acres of dramatic downland and beautiful beech woods with an extensive network of footpaths. The beech woods were planted in the 1920s by the Forestry Commission. Before then, the area was downland. The views from Butser Hill, the highest point on the South Downs at 270 metres (888ft), are among the finest in Southern England. In the beech woods there are wood-cutting displays, picnic and barbecue sites – and quiet glades where deer graze, butterflies dance and wood anemone, violets and wild orchids flourish. The park has been designated an Area of Outstanding Natural Beauty.

7. Return to the drive and cross diagonally left to join the Hangers Way and South Downs Way. Pass a parking area and skirt the lower edge of the wood. Reach a road and continue round the elbow to a gravel track on the right. Pass through a barbecue area and a barrier gate to enjoy a long straight walk through the beech hangers. Pass a second barbecue area and soon, a clearing where cycle tracks converge; 80 metres beyond the clearing reach a waymarked post on the left. Here, turn right (Hangers Way only) along a narrow, ascending path. Cross a wide track and bear left, descending gently. Leave the Country Park through a kissing-gate. Continue along the top edge of a field then gradually descend across two fields to a road. Cross the junction and continue along the Hangers Way, descending through pleasant woodland to a lane. Pass a picturesque thatched cottage with a fascinating assortment of guinea fowl, pheasants and peacocks in the garden; continue along the lane to Buriton pond.

7. Rowlands Castle

Route: No castle to explore – just a pleasant, easy ramble through undulating cornfields, meadows and light woodland. Good at any time of the year, but perfect in high summer when the village gardens are at their prettiest and the meadows are alive with an abundance of wild flowers.

Tea shop: **The Coffee Pot**, on The Green, offers a warm welcome to all ramblers. The varied menu includes an excellent range of home-made cakes, quiches and fruit pies – and a special, capacious 'group' teapot! There is seating in a pleasant garden. Open daily, 9.00am-5.00pm; Sundays in summer: 10.30am-6.00pm. Tel: 01705 412 538.

Distance: 4 miles.

How to get there: From the junction of the B2149 Horndean/Havant Road and the B2148, follow Redhill Road to Rowlands Castle. Turn left into Links Lane. At the village hall, turn right to the recreation ground.

Public Transport: Bus service: Hants & Sussex Motor Services. Trains: South West Trains.

Start: GR 730107.Rowlands Castle recreation ground (free).

Maps: Landranger 197; Explorer 120; Pathfinder 1285 SU61/71.

1. From the car park, turn left alongside the recreation ground. Turn left into 'The Peak'. Keep ahead through a gap in the hedge, from which the road continues to Greatfield Way. Here turn right to a junction then left along the road to Wellsworth Lane.

   Just before you turn off the road, a waymarked fingerpost is passed bearing a deer's-head symbol. This denotes The Staunton Way; a picturesque 12-mile linear walk from Queen Elizabeth Country Park, across the Downs, through Staunton Country Park and on to Langstone Harbour. These signs should not be confused with waymarks passed later for the Staunton Way Circular Walks; two easy walks of 2½ and 6 miles.

2. Turn right into Wellsworth Lane. The lane curves left at a house, 'The Barn' and continues, as a track, to a fork. Turn left by a thatched cottage, 'Wellsworth Farm' and ascend to the right for a

few metres to a field. Keep straight ahead through this large open field. Continue along a broad grassy path to a road. Turn right to descend to a junction. Cross over and turn left towards The George public house.

3. Just before reaching The George turn right over a stile into a field, immediately leave it by a stile on the left. Continue between fencing and shortly pass under a railway tunnel. Keep straight ahead, gently ascending, across a large open field. At the summit of the field an unmarked post by some trees denotes the boundary of Hampshire and West Sussex. From the post maintain the same direction, now descending, to a lane.

4. Turn left for a steady climb to South Holt Farm. Enter the farmyard, turn immediately right onto a broad track and descend to a junction. Cross onto a grassy path and climb through woodland to a field. Follow a line of telephone wires across the field to a stile. Over the stile, a narrow path leads to a drive and a road. Turn right along the road.

5. Immediately beyond an S-bend, at a sign for 'Forestside', turn left over a stile into a field. Keeping straight ahead, descend the field to a stile. Over the stile bear right to a stile into a copse. Follow a narrow path for 20 metres then turn right to meander through this long narrow copse. Leave the copse at a stile into a field. Cross to a stile on the right, then continue through a long narrow meadow. Cross a stile; after 20 metres fork right to skirt the bottom of the wood. Cross a stile and keep to the lower edge of the following two fields. Continue through light woodland and across an area of scrub to a track. Turn right to a road. Turn left to the village green and tea shop.

Rowlands Castle is dominated by the village green which sweeps through its centre in a long, broadening curve. Enclosing the green, at one end, is a large double viaduct; at the other end is a late 19th century flint Congregational Church. An attractive mixture of Georgian and Victorian buildings border the north side of the green. Flanking the south side is a long, old wall, behind which is a private house: in its grounds are the ivy-clad ruins of a small medieval castle. Little is known of the castle and its history remains obscure. The village grew from a hamlet during the 19th

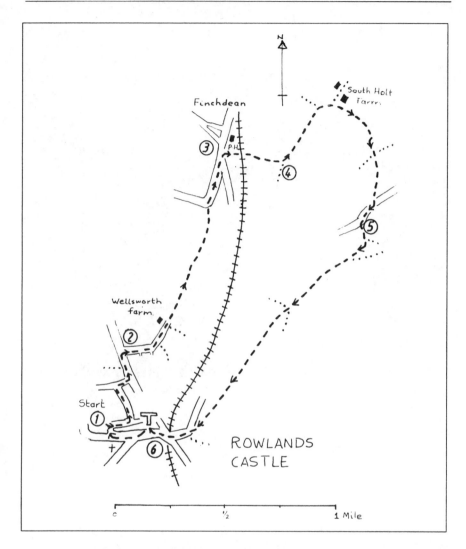

century, when it prospered from the brick-building industry and the construction of the London to Portsmouth railway, with a station at Rowlands Castle. Traditionally, two fairs had been held annually in the village, but these ceased early in the 19th century. Recently the tradition has been revived: a village fete, with craft stalls, brass bands, Maypole dancing and much more, is now held on the green each year in July.

'The Green'

6. Continue alongside the village green into Links Lane. Turn right opposite the village hall to return to the car park.

8. Hambledon & Broadhalfpenny Down

Route: A moderate walk across beautiful open countryside, with fieldpaths, farmtracks and quiet country lanes. The gentle climb to the summit of Broadhalfpenny Down gives amazing views over the rolling downland.

Tea shop: **Lott's General Store** is a typical village shop crammed with everyday essentials. In the tea shop, dried flowers hang from open timber beams and small pictures of local scenes, for sale, are temptingly arranged at eye level. The tea shop cosily seats eighteen and there is seating outside, where tea-drinkers and plants for sale, become part of the local scene. Sandwiches, home-made cakes and scones and a good pot of tea are all on the menu. It is open daily, 10.00am-4.30pm; Sundays in winter until 4.00pm. Tel: 01705 632 452.

Distance: 6½ miles.

How to get there: Hambledon is 9 miles south of Petersfield, signposted from the A3.

Public Transport: Bus services: Provincial Buses.

Start: GR 646151. Roadside parking in the High Street.

Maps: Landranger 185 & 196; Explorer 132; Pathfinder 1285 SU61/71.

Hambledon is known throughout the world as the cradle of cricket. A charming, very quiet village, it nestles under the protection of Windmill and Broadhalfpenny Downs. Figures in Domesday Book suggest a prosperous community existed at that time. Prosperity grew when Henry III granted the Bishop of Winchester a weekly market in Hambledon. In 1612, James I granted the right to two fairs a year. The letters patent were stamped with the word 'Broadhalfpenny' which was the toll paid to the Lord of the Manor for the setting up of booths.

The main street has a few beautiful half-timbered buildings, but it is the little High Street which attracts most attention. Backed by wooded slopes and lined with mainly Georgian buildings, the street climbs to the Parish Church and a view which has been captured many times in photographs and paintings. The church was once a

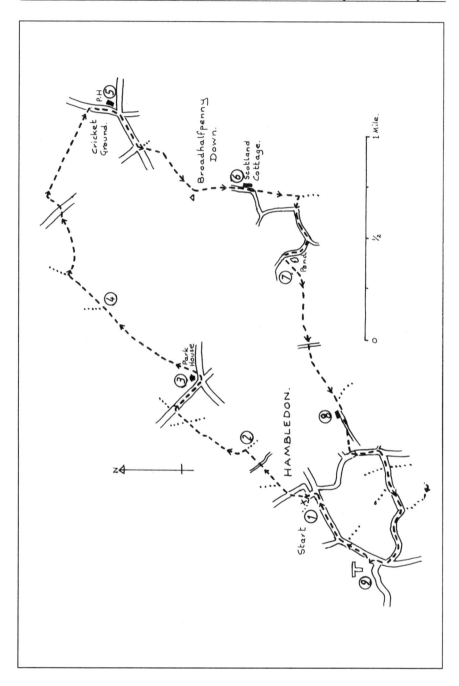

Saxon place of worship, and evidence of this can still be seen. The greatest surprise is the four exquisitely beautiful Norman arches in the centre of the church.

1. Walk up the High Street to the church. Pass through the gate and bear right through the church grounds to a road. Cross over, pass in front of the school then continue ahead between fields. Cross a track and pass a vineyard (part of Hambledon Vineyard) on the right.

2. Turn left onto a broad track, continue ahead along a narrow path to a stile. Over the stile bear left across a field to a stile at the bottom end of a hedgerow. Cross the stile and follow a narrow path between trees to a large open field. Bear left across the field: listen for the sound of the skylark 'a singing speck in the sky'. Reach a road and turn right to the main road. Turn left for 50 metres to Park House.

3. Turn left along the drive, pass through the metal gate ahead and follow a track alongside fields on your left. Continue ahead through pleasant light woodland for 220 metres to a waymarked post. (In summer the post is almost hidden in the undergrowth.) Here, fork left for 40 metres to a signpost at the edge of a field.

4. Fork diagonally right across the field to a waymarked post then turn right along the field edge. Turn left at a waymarked post to meander through a lovely ash plantation to a large open field. Turn right alongside the field to a lane. Cross over, go through a metal gate and follow a field boundary on your left to a stile. Turn right over the stile and walk through three fields which gently rise to the road. Turn right to walk down to the Bat & Ball public house.

Although cricket was not born in Hambledon, it was here on these downs, that it grew. The game matured one glorious day in 1777 when the village team took on the might of All England and beat them by an innings and 168 runs. Hambledon Cricket Club was formed in 1750 and soon rose to great heights; by 1770, it was established as the leading cricket club in England. Any rules passed became observed throughout the cricket world. The club established the width of the bat and introduced the middle stump. Previously some players had arrived with bats as wide as the stumps and bowlers had occasionally bowled right through the two stumps without displacing the bail! Spectators came from near and far. On one occasion a big match drew a crowd of over twenty thousand. The Bat & Ball Inn served as pavilion and club house. Richard Nyren, reputed to be the best all-round player of his day, was not only the captain, he was also the landlord of the inn. The team had attracted players from neighbouring counties. Due to the remoteness of Hambledon the best of these players found it increasingly easier to play nearer London. Eventually, the Marylebone Cricket Club was formed in 1787. A granite memorial to the club's early heroes has been erected on Broadhalfpenny Down opposite the Bat & Ball Inn.

Memorial to cricket at Hambledon

5. Turn right along the Hambledon road, but first look back to the amazing view of the downs and Windmill Hill. On reaching the Chidden road junction, turn left over a stile into a field. Bear slightly right to go quite steeply up the field to the stile on the right. Over the stile, turn right for the gentle ascent of Broadhalfpenny Down; first pause to admire the magnificent view across the wood-crowned

rolling downs. The track climbs to a height of 152 metres (502ft): at which point a gap in the trees allows a second view of Windmill Hill; whilst on the right, almost hidden in the trees, is a trig. point. From here the track descends to 'Scotland Cottage'.

6. Immediately beyond the cottage bear left between trees. The path soon opens up to give extensive views on the left. On reaching a junction, turn right along a track. As the track sweeps to the right, fork left; in 55 metres pass an electricity pole on the left. Turn right at a T-junction and soon reach a small pond on the left.

7. Turn left at the pond. Pass through a metal gate to an open barn on the left. Turn right uphill, crossing two stiles. From the second stile follow a line of electricity poles across three large open fields via stiles and a crossing track to a stile into a paddock.

8. Keep ahead through the paddock to a stile on the right. Continue to a drive and turn left. After 25 metres turn right along a fenced path. The path ends at a driveway to a house. Go down the drive to a lane. Turn left along the lane. On reaching a house, 'Little Rushmere', turn right and follow the quiet country lane for ½ mile as it twists and turns and eventually descends to the road. Turn right to Lott's General Store and Tea Shop.

9. From the tea shop continue along the road to a junction. Turn right to the village centre and the High Street.

9. Wickham and The Forest of Bere

Route: Well-made tracks, undulating woodland paths, Wickham Common and
                    pretty views. A pleasant walk for any season – during a dry spell. The
                    bridleway through Rookesberry Estate is usually quite muddy –
                    exceptionally so after rain.

Tea shop: **Bridge House Antique Centre & Tea Room** is in a delightful
                    Georgian Grade II listed building. An excellent array of cakes, scones
                    and light meals can be enjoyed either indoors or in the charming
                    courtyard garden overlooking the River Meon. Three floors of
                    fascinating antiques to browse around usually prove quite irresistible.
                    Open Tuesday to Sunday and Bank Holiday Mondays,
                    10.00am-5.00pm. Tel: 01329 833 079.

Distance: 5¼ miles.

How to get there: Wickham is at the junction of the A32 and B2177, 3 miles north of
                    Fareham.

Public Transport: Bus services: Stagecoach Hampshire Buses, Provincial Buses.

Start: GR 574116. Station Close car park (free) off Mill Lane, signposted
                    from 'The Square'.

Maps: Landranger 196; Explorer 119; Pathfinder 1284 SU 50/51.

Set in the beautiful Meon Valley and with a large, elegant square,
Wickham has been said to be the finest village in the south of England. The medieval square was built for 'tournies' (tournaments),
markets and an annual fair. Today it is flanked by attractive buildings from the 16th century, Georgian and Victorian times and the
20th century, all blending together in a surprisingly, harmonious
fashion. One of the earliest buildings, now a wine bar, has recently
uncovered an amazingly bright wall painting, circa 16th century.
The annual fair continues to this day, with a rare example of a traditional gypsies' horse fair.

Wickham's famous son was William Wykeham. Born in 1326 of
humble parents, he became Chancellor of England, Bishop of Winchester, builder of Winchester College and New College, Oxford,
and the inspirational architect of the remodelling of Winchester Ca-

thedral. One of the most admired men of his time, it has been said, 'Everything was done through him, and without him nothing was done.'

Early Victorian flint-gabled house in Bridge Street

1. From the car park turn right along the lane. At the end of a row of houses the lane becomes a track (once part of a railway line). Follow the track through a wood until reaching a railway bridge. Pass under the bridge, turn immediately left and climb the embankment. Cross the bridge and continue on a track, soon crossing a stream and then the River Meon. On reaching the main road, cross over to the grass verge and turn left: this is a very busy road and it is advisable to stay on the verge. Fifty metres beyond Chipphall Paddock, turn right into the Forest of Bere.

Saxon kings hunted here long before the Normans made Bere a Royal Forest. At one time the forest, a long swathe of some eight miles, stretched from King's Somborne to Rowland's Castle. Throughout the centuries timber was taken for shipbuilding; by the 17th century the woodland was reduced to 25 acres. However, in 1662, Samuel Pepys thought it so large and perilous that he 'hired a countryman to guide us to Havant to avoid going through the forest'. Today the forest is a haven for a rich diversity of wildlife. Birds of prey, crossbills and green wood-peckers nest in ancient oak and pine, while bluebells and over 63 species of other ancient woodland plants thrive in quiet secluded glades.

2. After 65 metres turn left: the path dips and rises as it leads straight through the wood to a 6-way junction. Here, continue ahead, passing a cycle track sign on your left. Ignore all paths off until reaching a 'Wood-end car park' sign. Here, turn left and go off-route to a small lily pond – a lovely, tranquil spot surrounded by birch and Scots pine.

3. Return to the track: 15 metres beyond the car park sign is a yellow waymarked post. Here make an acute right turn onto a narrow path; in 45 metres cross a small stream. Continue ahead at a crossing and gently ascend to a T-junction. Turn left onto a gravel track. After 70 metres turn right at a yellow waymarker. The path passes a narrow path on the left (hardly noticeable in summer) and curves right to a junction. Here bear left and ascend to the main track. Turn left along the track to reach West Walk car park, picnic area, and toilets.

4. Pass through the car park to the road. Turn right then right again into Rookesbury Estate. Although a narrow footpath runs parallel to the drive, it is easier to walk along the drive for 150 metres to a crossing path. Here, turn left onto a bridleway. This bridleway skirts the wood and follows the estate boundary for quite some time to the road – it is extremely muddy after rain. On reaching the driveway of the Estate, cross over to the continuation of the bridleway just in front of the entrance. You could leave the bridleway here and walk down the road, but there is no pavement. Follow the bridleway through until reaching the road. Turn right to a T-junction (B2177). Cross directly over and pass through a gate into Wickham Common.

5. Pass the countryside sign for Wickham Common and a wooden gate. Twelve metres beyond this gate turn right at a metal gate to cross the common. This is a lovely area, quiet and peaceful, with superb views. Follow the gorse hedgerow on your right across

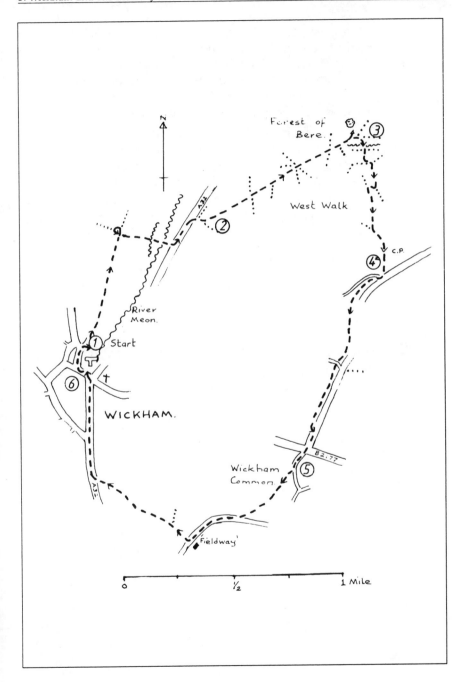

the common, pass under electrical cables and bear slightly right between oaks to a lane. Turn right along the lane. On reaching a bungalow 'Fieldway' turn right down a sunken track. The track continues, between large open fields, to a road (A32). Cross over and turn right along the road. At the roundabout, cross into School Road. Reach Bridge Street and turn left to Bridge House Antique Centre and Tea Room.

Before turning into Bridge Street, you will see a flight of steps leading to an ancient lattice bridge. From the bridge the track leads straight back to the car park. In Bridge Street, next to the Antique Centre, is the 19th century Chesapeake Mill. Timbers for its structure were bought in Portsmouth. They came from an American warship 'Chesapeake' captured by a British frigate 'Shannon' off Boston Harbour in 1813. In front of the mill is the well from which villagers drew water in the 1800s. Opposite the mill, set high in the wall of a row of picturesque half-timbered cottages, a plaque states 'Notice is hereby given that all vagrants found in or near this place will be apprehended and punished with the utmost severity the law will permit'.

6. From the tea room turn right then right again into Mill Lane to return to the car park.

10. Bishop's Waltham

Route: A pleasant walk through light, varied woodland and across open fields.
                   Two gentle climbs give rise to extensive views. The walk ends at the
                   picturesque ruins of Bishop's Waltham Palace.

Tea shop: **The Palm Tree Coffee Shop** is a little gem hidden away at the back of
                   the gift shop in the King's Christian Centre. The dining area is prettily
                   decorated with bamboo, canework and palm trees. Light lunches and
                   an assortment of home-made cakes and scones are served by friendly
                   volunteer helpers. Open Monday-Saturday, 9.15am-5.30pm.
                   Tel: 01489 893 877.

Distance: 6 miles.

How to get there: Bishop's Waltham is on the B2177, 4 miles north of Wickham.

Public Transport: Bus Services: Stagecoach Hampshire Bus, Provincial Buses, Solent
                   Blue Line.

Start: GR 553176. Lower Lane car park (pay & display).

Maps: Landranger 185; Explorer 119; Pathfinder 1284 (SU50/51).

Bishop's Waltham was plain Waltham until the year 904, when it was swapped by Edward the Elder to the Bishop of Winchester in exchange for land at Portchester. The town suffered major destruction at the hands of the marauding Danes. It recovered under William the Conqueror and at the time of the Domesday Survey 'several mills and two places of worship' were recorded. The village was one of many used for imprisoning French captives during the Napoleonic Wars. In more recent times, a local firm, Blanchard's Brickworks, supplied bricks for the construction of Blackfriars Bridge in London and the Suez Canal.

Today, Bishop's Waltham is a charming mostly Georgian town, with a few half-timbered buildings and narrow picturesque streets. Its prettiest street is perhaps St Peter's which, lined with ivy-clad Georgian houses and wisteria-covered cottages, climbs to the 12th century, flint parish church.

1. From the car park cross over into Bank Street. (The medieval

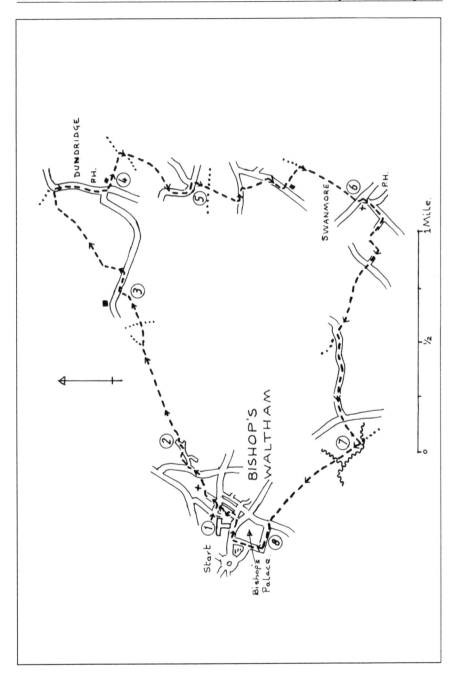

house on the corner was reconstructed in 1998 by a local resident). Turn first left into St Peter's Street. Bear right through the church grounds to a road. Turn left along the road. On reaching Colville Drive cross over to a path on its left, parallel to the main road. At the end of the path continue along a lane to reach (the middle of) Colville Drive. Turn left. At the end of the drive turn right along a passage between houses.

2. Pass through a kissing-gate into a field. Go diagonally right across two fields to a stile in a hedgerow. Over the stile turn right along a narrow path. After 65 metres fork right to enter a wood. The path rises and falls as it meanders through this long narrow wood. Shortly ignore a crossing path with steps up and down. Eventually a modern house can be seen ahead, over to the left, through the trees. When the house is immediately on your left, find a stile 10 metres to the left, down a slight incline.

3. Cross the stile into a field. Follow a right-hand boundary to a lane. Turn right. After 100 metres turn left into a field. Follow a left-hand boundary for 140 metres then bear right across the field. Maintain the same direction, gently ascending to a panoramic view, across the next two fields. Turn right alongside a field boundary to a lane. Turn right along the lane. Pass the Hampshire Bowman public house and continue ahead to Galley Down Farm.

4. Turn left through the farmyard to a stile on the left of a farm cottage. Cross three paddocks to a stile at the right-hand side of the third paddock. Turn right along a woodland path. After 35 metres fork left onto a bridleway; ascend Damson Hill and emerge at a road. Turn left along the road. At a junction turn right for 15 metres to a stile on the right into a field. From here there are fine views southwesterly to Fawley and Southampton and west to Bishop's Waltham.

5. Follow the left-hand boundary down the field to a farm track. Turn left and cross diagonally to a stile on the right. Follow a right-hand field boundary to a lane. Turn right along the lane. Reach Dolphin Cottage and turn left along a narrow path. Enter a field and follow the right-hand hedgerow for 20 metres then bear

slightly left across the field to a stile at the end of the hedgerow. A fenced path leads to a road.

6. Turn left and cross into New Road. Turn right along Broad Lane, a long lane which degenerates into an unmade lane. Eventually cross a road and continue ahead to join a grassy track. Pass through a kissing-gate and continue ahead alongside a right-hand boundary, then between hedgerows, to enter a copse. Continue ahead through the copse, pass through a small clearing on the right and soon reach a lane. Turn left along the lane. Cross the B2177 and follow a short path into a field. Cross the field to a footbridge – don't cross it – instead turn right to reach a footbridge in the far corner of the field. The streams in these meadows form a source of the River Hamble.

7. Over the bridge cross the field and pass through a squeeze stile made from old railway lines. Follow a right-hand boundary uphill, across two fields, pass through another squeeze stile and descend to a road. Cross diagonally left to Bishop's Lane.

Bishop Waltham's Palace

Bishop's Waltham Palace was built as a castle in 1136 by Bishop Henry de Blois (see walk 1). Two hundred years later it was made into a palace by William of Wykeham (walk 9), who lived in it for 3 years until his death in 1404. During the Middle Ages the Bishops of Winchester were rich and powerful; their grand palaces became the venue of many important royal occasions. In 1189 Richard the Lionheart stayed at the palace after his coronation at Winchester; Henry V was a guest after his victory at Agincourt and in 1522 Henry VIII and Charles of Spain signed a 'Treaty of Bishop's Waltham' here. The palace was destroyed by the Parliamentarians during the Civil War. Today, under the care of English Heritage, it is a picturesque, moated ruin set in attractive grounds. Its remains include a three-storey tower and the soaring windows of Wykeham's great hall. For further information tel: 01489 892 460.

8. The lane descends to the palace entrance. Just before reaching the entrance cross over to the Town Square. Continue along High Street to the tea shop. From the tea shop turn left into Bank Street to return to the car park.

11. Botley & Manor Farm Country Park

Route: An easy walk through farmland, woodland and along the River
                    Hamble, with the opportunity to visit an interesting, traditional farm and
                    museum.

Tea shop: **The Pantry Tea Room** at Manor Farm serves an enticing assortment
                    of home-made puddings, cakes and scones, with a lunch menu
                    ranging from a bacon sandwich to a full roast. There are picnic tables
                    in a pleasant courtyard. The tea room can be visited without paying for
                    entrance to the farm. It is open the same times as the farm,
                    Easter-October, daily 10.00am-5.00pm. November-Easter, Sundays
                    only 10.00am-dusk. Closed first & last Sunday of each year.
                    Tel: 01489 787 055.

Distance: 4 ¾ miles.

How to get there: Botley is on the A334. Leave the M27 at junction 7.

Public Transport: Bus services: Solent Blue Line, Provincial Buses. Trains: South West
                    Trains.

Start: GR 511131. Mortimer Road car park (free).

Maps: Landranger 196; Pathfinder 1284 SU50/51; Outdoor Leisure 22.

Botley is an attractive market town, granted its Royal Charter in 1267. William Cobbett, the town's most famous resident, described it as 'The most delightful village in the world...the soil was rich...and it had neither attorney nor a justice of the peace.' Here he combined his radical journalism with successful farming. From here also, he was fined £1,000 and sentenced to two years imprisonment for his outcries against the treatment of British soldiers. They had each been given 500 lashes for protesting (strongly) against reductions in their pay.

At one time barges came up the River Hamble to Botley Flour Mill. The mill still stands: today it houses speciality shops and a tea shop (it closes at 3.30pm). There are plans to open part of the mill as a working museum. From the latter part of the 19th century, Botley was famous for its high quality strawberries: these are still grown to-day, though perhaps not in such large quantities. The High Street has some attractive Georgian and Edwardian buildings. The Market Hall (1848) was built with funds from the Botley Farmers' Club which was founded by William Cobbett.

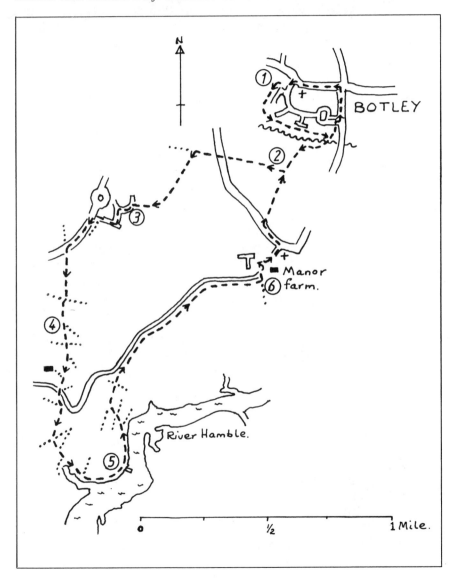

1. From the rear of the car park follow a footpath to playing fields and turn left alongside them. At the end of the fields turn left to walk between a housing development on the left and a common on the right. On reaching house no.16, cross the common and turn left along a riverside path. Soon cross a footbridge and ascend to a kissing-gate. Turn right for 10 metres then left along a grassy track. Pass through a gate and keep ahead across a strawberry field. Pass into another field and turn left alongside the hedgerow for 60 metres to a waymarker.

2. Here turn right and go straight across the field to a road. Cross onto a path opposite and continue between hedgerows. Shortly pass under electricity cables; 18 metres beyond the cables turn left along a narrow path with wire fencing on the right. Ignore a path at the end of the fencing and continue through scrub. Reach a gravel track parallel to a recreation park. Continue alongside the park, pass through a metal gate and keep ahead to a road.

3. Turn left then left again into Salwey Road. At the T-junction follow Ambleside round to the right. At the end of Ambleside, nine steps lead to a road. Turn left along the road – a busy road so make good use of the grass verge. After 200 metres turn left into Tanhouse Lane. At a crossing take a path parallel to the drive to Cricketwood: the path leads into Manor Farm Country Park.

   The park comprises 400 acres of scenic farmland, ancient woodland and saltmarsh. In times past, oak from the woods was used for naval shipbuilding and hazel and ash coppiced for hurdles, thatching spars and faggots. Today, an intricate network of paths allow quiet exploration of the woodland and lead, sooner or later, to the upper reaches of the River Hamble.

4. Pass the Country Park sign and descend through woodland. Ignore all paths off and shortly pass the entrance to Queen Elizabeth II Activity Centre. Thirty metres beyond the entrance, bear left at a waymarked post to a road. Cross the road into the wood and bear left at the first junction. Ignore paths off and soon reach a broad track. Here, turn right, immediately passing a path left to the public toilets and picnic area. The track meanders through

the wood, passes a footbridge on the right then continues along the bank of the Hamble.

The largest ship ever built in medieval times, the 'Grace De Dieu' was built on the Hamble. In 1439, because of a mutinous crew, the ship was returned to its moorings. During a fierce storm lightning struck and the ship caught fire. Although some of the ship was saved, and the wood reused, most of it was beyond rescue and is still under water. At very low tide part of the ship's structure can be seen from the landing stage.

5. Reach a signpost and continue towards Manor Farm: you may like to digress for a while and enjoy the views of the river from the landing stage, or from various access points along the way. Ignore two crossing paths and leave the wood at a road. Turn right onto a track parallel to the road and with open countryside on the right. The track is signposted 'Tea Room' but be patient; it's still almost ¾ mile away.

One acre of corn, in the cornfields passed en route to the tea room, is farmed using traditional methods. The corn is cut by a mechanical

Sheaves of corn stacked in stooks at Manor Farm

reaper, circa early 1900s, tied loosely in bundles (sheaves), then stacked and left to dry; each stack of eight sheaves is called a stook. When dry, the corn is collected by horse-drawn carts. The farm has a variety of activities to delight young children and much to take (older) mums and dads back a year or two. You can learn 'by rote' in the Victorian schoolroom and help with the feeding of young farm animals. Most activities are on specific days. For further information tel: 01489 787 055.

Behind the farm is St Bartholomew's church, a charming 13th century chancel, it is the remains of the old parish church and is used today for special services only.

6. Leave the farm by the gate opposite the farm shop and turn right towards the church. Pass the church on the right and join a road. Turn left along the road. At the end of the garden wall of 'The Old Rectory' turn right into a field. Follow the right-hand boundary to the strawberry field crossed earlier in the walk and retrace the route to the footbridge over the stream. Cross the bridge and ascend ahead. At the road turn right to a junction. Turn left along a lane. Turn left into High Street. Immediately beyond the parish church turn left into Mortimer Road.

12. Hamble &
The Royal Victoria Country Park

Route: A varied route with roads, fields, a country park, a shingle beach, the
                       River Hamble and a picturesque village. A pleasant, interesting walk;
                       enjoyable at any time of the year.

Tea shop: Three hundred years ago coffins were made in the loft of what is now
                       Hamble Village Tea Room. The pulley used for pulling up timber, and
                       lowering the finished coffins, can be seen on the wall outside. Today
                       the tea room is a friendly meeting place; the loft now houses overflow
                       diners. The menu offers early breakfast (for overnighting sailors!), light
                       lunches and delicious home-made cakes and scones. There is an
                       attractive tea-garden. It is open all year except Christmas Day.
                       Easter-October, 7.30am-6.00pm. Winter, 9.00am-4.00pm.
                       Tel: 01703 455 583.

                       The Empire Tea Room in the Country Park serves light lunches and
                       home-made cakes. It is open every day Easter-September,
                       10.30am-5.00pm. October-November, weekends only – opening hours
                       depend on the weather! Tel: 01703 457745.

Distance: 5 ¾ miles.

How to get there: Hamble is on the B3397, signposted from the M27 at junction 8.

Public Transport: Bus services: Solent Blue Line.

Start: GR 483068. Hamble Square car park (free).

Maps: Landranger 196; Outdoor Leisure 22.

---

1. From the car park turn right along the road. Turn right into Hamble House Gardens. At the end of the road continue ahead through a children's playground. Bear left through birch to a fenced path: this long pleasant path ends at a road. Turn left along the road: it is a busy road and there is no verge, take care.

2. After ¼ mile, as the road turns left, pass through a barrier gate onto a track. Soon cross a railway bridge and continue ahead between chain-link fencing. On reaching a concrete driveway cross

diagonally right onto a woodland path. After 75 metres turn left by a large oak tree. At a sign for Mallards Moor turn left to a stile. From the stile continue ahead, crossing the open moor to a road.

3. Turn left along the road (B3397). At a junction turn right into Hound Road. Pass St Mary's church and turn left through a kissing-gate into Hound Corner Ecology Park. Follow the permissive path through the park to a further kissing-gate to a road. Turn left to reach the Royal Victoria Country Park. Follow the road through the park until reaching a crossing with various directional signs. Cross the road, signed 'Pay and Display', to a narrow gravel path which leads to the tea room and the chapel.

The Country Park covers 200 acres of scenic woodland and open grassland, with ¾ mile of shoreline. The Royal Victoria Hospital was built in 1856 for the care of soldiers from the Crimean War. However, Florence Nightingale disapproved. It was the first Army Hospital in Great Britain and had been built for grandeur, not for the comfort of the wounded. The 434 metre (1424ft) long frontage ran parallel to Southampton Water, but there was no 'sea view' for the patients – all the ward windows were at the back of the building, overlooking the outhouses. In its day, the hospital was one of the longest buildings in the world. The hospital chapel is all that survives, it is now a museum. The 30 metre (100ft) high tower allows spectacular views of the surrounding countryside and the Isle of Wight. For further information, tel: 01703 455 157.

4. From the chapel walk down to the remains of the hospital pier and turn left along the shingle beach. Reach the second slipway and turn onto a narrow path: this path is easier on the feet; it follows the shoreline with viewpoints and seats at various intervals and finally drops down to the beach again. Pass the oil depot and turn onto the path which skirts the common, still following the shoreline, to Hamble Point Marina and the road.

5. Cross over to a tree-lined footpath – don't go through the kissing-gate. Keep parallel with the road until reaching a signpost for Hamble Village. Turn right. At a junction continue towards the village: the path returns to the shoreline then bears left over a plank footbridge. Continue through woodland to a car park. Turn right towards the Hamble.

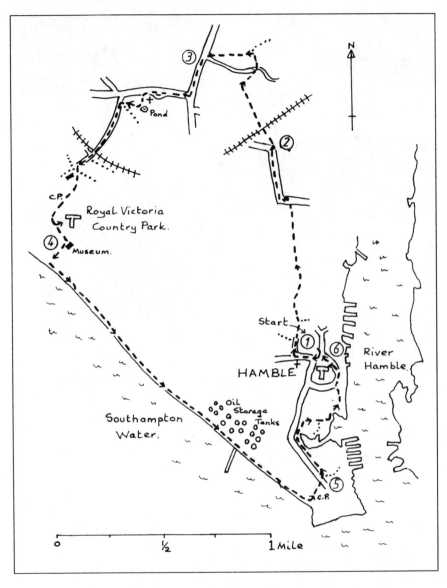

Over many centuries the River Hamble proved a convenient landing stage for the enemies of England. The Saxons gained their first foothold on the island here. A century or so later came the longships of the marauding Danes, who pillaged and ravaged their way to Winchester. In 1345,

The tea shop, Hamble

Hamble proved its own worth by providing 7 ships and 117 men for the battle fought and won against the French at Crecy. In 1377, the village and port were devastated by the French raiders. Justice was finally done 400 years later when over 2,000 French prisoners from the Napoleonic Wars were brought ashore at Hamble before being marched off to prisons throughout Hampshire.

In more peaceful times Hamble was an active fishing port and earned its living from lobsters, oysters and crab from the Solent. Today the village thrives as a busy, picturesque yachting centre and is threatened by nothing more than a major influx of tourists during the summer months. The winding, climbing High Street, from which it gained the name Hamble-le-Rice (Hamble Rise), is flanked by small, attractive 17th century and Georgian houses, one of which is the village tea room.

6. Continue along High Street to the tea room and beyond to the car park.

---

13. Exbury and The Solent

Route: Fieldpaths, light woodland and an interesting coastal walk with superb
                     views. There are two possible stops: Lepe Country Park is a beautiful
                     spot – the ideal place for a swim on a hot sunny day; Exbury Gardens
                     are glorious in any season.

Tea shop: The former blacksmith's forge at Exbury Gardens, has been skilfully
                     converted into **The Smithy Tea Room**. Thoughtfully, it has a
                     wood-burning stove for those chilly days. The self-service counter
                     offers a good range of light lunches and home-made cakes and
                     scones. There are picnic tables outside, temptingly placed within sight
                     of the plant centre! The tea room can be visited without paying for the
                     gardens. It is open daily: March-1st November, 10.00am-5.30pm.
                     Tel: 01703 898 737.

                     Lepe Bay Restaurant is a licensed café in an idyllic setting in the
                     Country Park. Light lunches, home-made soup and an excellent range
                     of home-made cakes are served by friendly assistants. It is open daily:
                     April-October, 10.30am-5.30pm. November-March, 10.30am-dusk,
                     weekends only. Tel: 01703 893 681.

Distance: 5 ¾ miles.

How to get there: From Beaulieu take the B3054 for one mile. Turn right then right again
                     to Exbury. Turn left through the village. At the first fork bear left (signed
                     Blackfield) for one mile to the car park.

Public Transport: Bus service: Solent Blue Line.

Start: GR 433013. Darkwater Car Park. If using public transport the walk will
                     begin at Exbury Gardens.

Maps: Outdoor Leisure 22; Landranger 196.

---

1. From the car park turn right along the road for ½ mile; there is no
    verge and an S-bend has to be negotiated, so take care. Ignore a
    footpath at Sturt Cottage and continue to an elbow. Here turn left
    over a stile along a grassy path. Fifteen metres before the path
    curves left, turn right along a grassy path with trees left and fields
    right. Continue ahead between oak, elderberry and hawthorn to

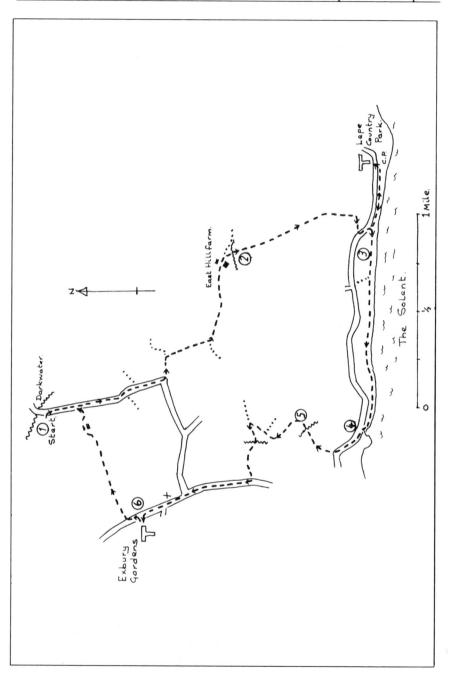

a gate to an unsurfaced road. Turn left along the road. On reaching Easthill Farm turn right through the farmyard. Turn right again, between the two brick walls at the end of the farmyard, into a field. Bear left downhill to a footbridge then gently ascend to a field.

2. Follow waymarks straight across this field and then a small field. Cross a large field heading to the right of a wood, then keep ahead and pass by the second electricity pole, counting from the left of the field. Cross a stile and bear slightly right to a further stile. Keep ahead to cross a footbridge then bear right to leave the field at the top corner. Turn left along a road: in two minutes, reach the Solent and superb views to the Isle of Wight.

If refreshments are needed, turn left along the coastal path to Lepe Country Park. During the Second World War, sections of the 'Mulberry' harbours were made here before being towed to Normandy during the D-Day invasions of 1944. Today, pine trees and lawn sweep down to the shore, ships and sails glide by and scenic coastal walks can be enjoyed.

3. Turn right for a ¾ mile coastal walk. At the end of the groynes cross a rough grassy patch and continue through scrub, with a wire fence on the left. It next becomes necessary to negotiate a number of fallen trees – quite an exciting process when the tide is in! Once the trees are passed, enjoy the tranquillity of the salt

Groynes along the coastal path

marshes and the rich variety of wading birds. The coastal path ends at a stile to a road.

4. Turn left along the road. Reach an elbow and turn right onto a gravel track. Pass immediately through a kissing-gate onto a tree-lined path, a welcome summer glade. Continue through light woodland, crossing a plank footbridge and, bearing left, gently ascending to a further plank footbridge.

5. Cross the footbridge into a large field. Turn left alongside a hedgerow: pass a wide gap and turn left with the hedgerow and continue alongside it as it curves round the field to a stile. From the stile keep to the woodland on your left across two fields, turning left at the second field, to reach a T-junction. Here turn left. The path skirts the wood then meanders through it via a footbridge and a right turn. Emerge at a field with good views on the left towards the Isle of Wight. Go straight across the field to a road. Turn right: keep ahead at a junction to reach Exbury Gardens and the tea room.

Exbury Gardens were created in the 1920s by Lionel de Rothschild. One hundred and fifty men were employed. A private railway was constructed to transport rocks for the rockery and wells dug so that water was always available for the million or so new plants. At the end of ten years, 200 acres of forest had been transformed into a garden of breathtaking beauty. Finance was provided for plant-hunting expeditions to collect the seeds of rare plants – especially rhododendrons; Rothschild's favourite plants. In time, over 1,200 new hybrids of rhododendrons and azaleas were bred. Today, one can gaze in wonder at daffodil meadows – stunning spring displays of rhododendrons, azaleas and camellias, summer rose gardens and amazing autumn colours reflected in deep, still waters. Little wonder that Exbury is considered to be one of the finest woodland gardens in the world. It is open from 1 March–1 November. For further information tel: 01703 891 203.

6. From the tea room continue down the road to the exit gates of the Gardens. Turn right over a stile along a track between large open fields. Eventually pass a farmhouse on the right and continue to the road. Turn left to return to the car park.

14. Milford-on-Sea. Keyhaven & Hurst Castle

Route: Diverse, level terrain with fields, woodland, coastal paths and a Tudor castle. Marvellous for a clear day, when there are unrivalled views to the Isle of Wight and a ferry trip to Hurst Castle can be enjoyed.

Tea shop: From a large selection we have chosen two. The **Milford Patisserie** and **Wizard's Kitchen** is a combined patisserie and tea shop. Excellent home cooked lunches and cream teas are served in a cosy dining room decorated with original paintings and sculptured mystic figures. The new owners are currently landscaping the garden and building a conservatory for dining in. Open daily in summer, 9.00am-5.30pm. Winter until 4.00pm, Monday-Saturday, half-day Wednesday. Tel: 01590 645 052.

The Marine Café, with tables outside, is ideally placed at the end of the shingle spit for those still wishing to breathe in the sea air whilst 'taking tea'. Hot meals, a variety of cakes, a good choice of drinks, and ice cream can be obtained. Open daily from 9.00am-5.00pm, April to October. Weekends only from November to March and closed all December and early January. Tel: 01590 642 150.

Distance: 7 miles (6 miles if not taking the ferry).

How to get there: Milford-on-Sea is on the B3058, 3½ miles south of Lymington. The car park is signposted from the village green.

Public Transport: Bus service: Wilts & Dorset. Ferry: a service to Hurst Castle operates daily from April to the end of October. At other times a limited service operates, subject to weather and tide conditions. For further information tel: 01590 642 500.

Start: GR 291918. Sea Road car park (free).

Maps: Landranger 195 or 196; Outdoor Leisure 22.

Milford-on-Sea has a delightful position on the southern coastline. Westward wild Hengistbury Head can be seen. Ahead the sun sets over the Isle of Wight. Milford has grown as a seaside resort since the 1800s, the words 'on-Sea' being added in 1880. The large village

green, now the venue for fairs and carnivals, is the last remains of
what was an extensive area of common land.

North of the green, the 13th century parish church has hardly
changed over the years. It is reputed to be one of the most distinctive
of small churches in Hampshire. One of its more recent features is a
glass window commemorating the time Charles I was held prisoner
in Hurst Castle.

Danestream, by the village car park, marks the beginning of the
Solent Way, a 61-mile walk along the Hampshire seaboard, with a
stretch through the New Forest, to Emsworth.

1. From the car park return to the road, turn right over Danestream
   to the High Street. Cross over at the junction and walk up Church
   Hill. Pass the pretty thatched cottage overlooking the green and
   continue up the lane to the parish church. Turn right to the main
   road. Turn left for 250 metres to a pillar-box set in the remains of
   a brick wall.

2. Turn right onto a path signposted 'Lymore': as you enter a field
   there are marvellous views ahead across the Solent. Follow the
   left-hand boundary until it turns left, then keep ahead to an
   elaborate signpost in the middle of the field. Here, bear left towards Lymore. At the edge of the field turn right, keep the edge of
   a copse on your left for 50 metres then bear left through the copse
   to a road. Cross the road and turn left into Lymore Lane. On
   reaching a house 'The Mount', turn right then immediately left
   along a narrow ascending path.

3. Cross a stile and go diagonally across three fields. In mid-
   September with the corn 'as high as an elephant's eye' it was a joy
   to discover the rights-of-way had been kept very clear. At the
   start of the third field a signpost points the way to Efford Bridge.
   On leaving this field turn left along a grassy path.

4. Where the path turns left, turn right into a field (signposted 'E-
   fford Bridge'). Follow the left-hand boundary for 15 metres then
   head slightly right towards a wood, passing immediately to the
   left of an electricity pole. Enter the wood at the corner, via a stile
   almost hidden in the trees. The path, never far from the grounds
   of Efford Experimental Horticulture Station on the left, mean-

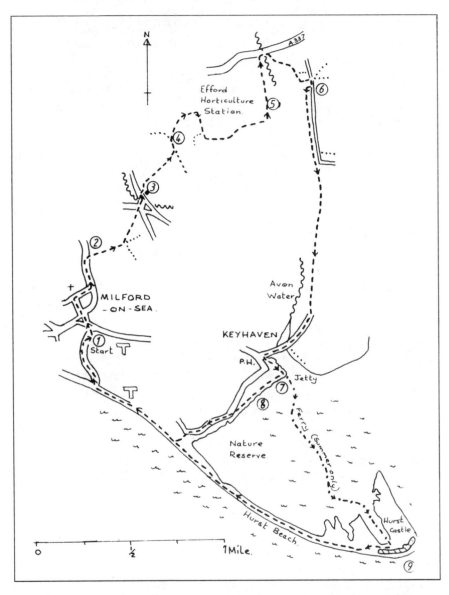

ders through the wood to a crossing track at the gates to the Station. Cross the track and continue ahead. At the end of the Station grounds the path continues deeper into the wood.

5. Leave the wood via a stile and follow a left-hand boundary across two fields to a road. Turn right. Just after crossing Avon Water turn right along a gravel track. The track gently rises and sweeps round to a waymarked stile on the right. Cross the stile and follow a left-hand field boundary to a further waymarked stile. Over the stile turn right and follow the field boundary to a road. Turn right for 25 metres then enter a field.

6. The path now continues, parallel to the road, through several fields and although there is the constant noise of a re-cycling station on the left, this is more than compensated for as the Solent and the Isle of Wight come into view. At the end of the fields keep forward along a broad gravel track. This track leaves the road and continues between fields. Soon pass a landfill site on the left and continue between scrub to a road. Keep ahead to Keyhaven Harbour.

The harbour is a lovely spot in which to while away time. The views are splendid, yachts and the little ferry bob busily to and fro, birds dip and dive across the marshes – and the old Gun Inn offers the same friendly welcome to yachtsmen and walkers alike. Keyhaven Marshes have provided salt, by sea water evaporation, since Saxon times. In the 1700s, there were five salt-works at Milford and Keyhaven. By 1850, heavy taxes and competition had led to the death of this local industry. The marshes now provide habitat for herons, curlews, oyster-catchers and many more water-fowl.

7. Follow the harbour wall round to the ferry stage on the far side for the short journey over the water to Hurst Castle.

Hurst Castle was built between 1541 and 1544 to guard the western end of the Solent. Comprising a twelve-sided tower with a 3-bastion wall, it is said to be Henry VIII's most sophisticated artillery fort. Extensive modernisation took place throughout the Napoleonic Wars. Its strength was again increased during the late 1800s. It was occupied by the Parliamentarians during the Civil War and in December 1648 was a temporary prison for Charles I before being taken to London for trial and execution. Records show it is unlikely the castle ever had the full quota of weapons designed for it. However, during both world wars its batteries of quick-firing guns were deemed adequate to guard against surface raiders and

Hurst Castle and lighthouse

aircraft. The castle is well worth visiting, if only to see the two massive muzzle guns on show. Each gun used shells weighing over 800 lbs. and took twelve men to operate.

8. Those not wishing to take the ferry should continue alongside the harbour wall then follow the embankment between the salt marshes to the road. Cross over to an embankment and continue ahead. Cross a footbridge and climb the embankment of the shingle spit.

9. From the Castle, turn left to Hurst Spit: a narrow bank of shingle magnificently stabilised with groynes and boulders. This two-mile walk along the spit is quite beautiful. On the right, is the lovely, peaceful harbour with its quiet inlets and pretty yachts. On the left, the sea and the marvellous views back to the Isle of Wight and the Needles, are the perfect excuse for many stops along the way. At the end of the spit is the **Marine Café**. Continue along the sea road. Turn right opposite **The Needles Café** into Sea Road to return to Milford, more teashops and the car park. At the High Street turn right to **The Milford Wizard**!

15. Brockenhurst and Aldridge Hill Inclosure

Route: Open commons, woodland, picturesque Ober Water, and a gentle
                        climb across wild open heathland – a beautiful walk with extensive
                        views. An OS map and a compass are advisable.

Tea shop: Brockenhurst has two main tea shops, both serve excellent
                        home-cooked meals and delicious cakes and scones – yes, we did go
                        in each one! **The Brock & Bruin**, apart from badgers and bears galore
                        around its walls, is a traditional tea shop. It is open all year from
                        10.00am-6.00pm. Tel: 01590 622 020.

                        Splashes is a small confectionery and card shop with a tiny, very
                        pretty, dining area at its rear – there is also a small courtyard. It is open
                        daily Easter to October, 9.00am-5.00pm. Winter; Monday to Friday,
                        10.00am-2.00pm and Saturday, 10.00am-5.00pm. Tel: 01590 622 120.

Distance: 5¼ miles.

How to get there: Brockenhurst is on the A337, 3 miles south of Lyndhurst.

Public Transport: Bus service: Wilts & Dorset. Trains: South West Trains.

Start: GR 299023. Village car park. Free with a long stay area at the far end.

Maps: Outdoor Leisure 22; Landranger 195 & 196.

Bordered by wide open lawns, Brockenhurst is set in the heart of the
New Forest. Its name is Saxon, meaning Badger's Wood: the word
'lawn' is the New Forest name for open areas of grazing. The 'Beeching Axe' was avoided here; trains still cross the main street at a
Continental-style crossing. Ponies graze on the village green, paying
little attention to the passing traffic.

The parish church is the oldest in the New Forest: a yew tree in its
grounds is said to pre-date the forest itself. The graveyard contains a
memorial to over 100 New Zealand soldiers from the First World
War who died in the field hospitals near Brockenhurst. Also here is
the grave of Harry 'Brusher' Mills – a snake-catcher who lived for 30
years as a hermit in the forest. Most of the adders he caught were
sold to zoos as food for other snakes. His nickname arose from his
enthusiasm for sweeping Lyndhurst cricket pitch between innings –
necessary because of the continuous encroachment of ponies.

Ponies grazing on the heathland

1. From the car park, turn right to walk through the village. Turn right along Rheinfield Road, first alongside a stream then the green. At Meerut Road, turn right then immediately left onto a gravel path to traverse Butt's Lawn – a large open common. Cross two footbridges then, ten metres before a wooden seat set in concrete, turn left to a solitary tree and a gravel path just beyond.

2. Where the path turns left to circle a copse, turn right onto a narrow path and walk alongside the copse, keeping it on your left. When the path forks left through the copse to a caravan site, continue ahead, still keeping the copse on your left. On reaching the road to the caravan site, turn right. Continue along the road as it curves left at Ober Corner.

3. On reaching a Forestry Commission sign for Aldridge Hill turn right. Within a few metres cross a footbridge over Ober Water. Turn left at Aldridgehill Cottage: here a small stone on the left is inscribed with dates of the inclosure periods.

    Aldridge Hill was first enclosed in 1681. It was opened to grazing in 1983. Most of the mature trees in the area have grown from natural and planted seedlings following felling in the First World War. However, close

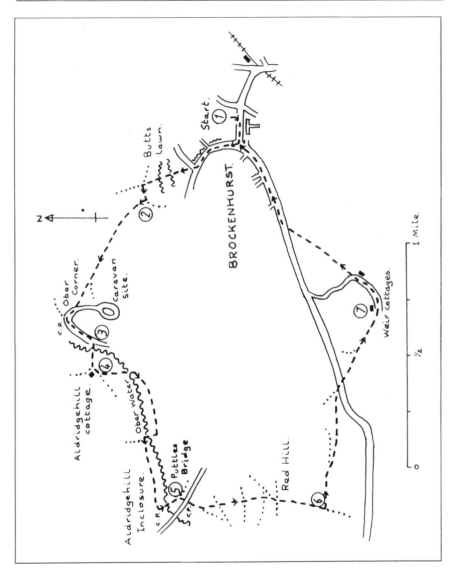

to Ober Water a stretch of ancient open woodland has developed natu-
rally. The whole area presents a rich habitat for flora and fauna. Purple
moor grass, bog myrtle, yellow-flowered bog asphodel and the insectivo-
rous sundew all thrive in the boggy areas and the picturesque stream
has become a popular watering-hole for cattle, deer and ponies.

4. Ten metres beyond the stone, fork left into Aldridge Hill Inclosure. Shortly cross a wooden footbridge over Ober Water. Turn right at the red waymarked post to follow Ober Water on your right. At a junction turn right over a wooden footbridge then immediately left to follow the path to Puttles Bridge car park.

5. Cross Puttles Bridge and continue along the gravel track, parallel to the road. Shortly turn right and cross the road to Puttles Pines car park sign. Take the broad grassy path behind the sign, noting the pine plantation over to the right, but keeping to the broad path. One hundred metres beyond the plantation take a left fork, heading south towards Red Hill on a very gently ascending path. Keep ahead at three crossing paths. Immediately beyond the third crossing a broad grassy path merges from the left. Here the path bears slightly right and in 25 metres crosses a narrow path to reach the summit. On a clear day there are superb views left across the heathland with Brockenhurst in the distance. From the summit, descend between gorse. As the path levels out and widens and the gorse becomes more sparse, look for a well-worn track on the left running parallel to the road. At this point, the road is about ¼ mile ahead.

6. Turn left along the track. After ¼ mile, at a large patch of gorse, fork right onto a narrow path which leads diagonally to the road and six small barrier posts. Cross over and take a path behind two small barrier posts. The path bears slightly left and heads towards a single redbrick and white-painted building with two white chimneys. As the path merges with a track from the left, continue ahead.

7. Turn left in front of the building, now seen as Weir Cottages. When the lane turns left at a house, The Upper Ford, continue ahead along a gravel track. Pass through two kissing-gates into a field and follow a fence on the left to two further kissing-gates into a field. Cross ahead to a stile and follow a fenced path, with a stream on the right, to a farm. Keep alongside the farmyard to a stile and the road. Turn right along the road. Cross over at Armstrong Lane to a gravel path which skirts the road to the village. Cross back into Brookley Road to the tea shops and the car park.

16. Holmsley, Wilverley Inclosure and The Naked Man

Route: Meadows, streams, woodland and wild, heather-covered, heathland. This is the New Forest at its best – except, possibly after heavy rain, when the wood at the end of the walk can be quite boggy.

Tea shop: Rescued from dereliction in the 1970s, the old station waiting room now thrives as a warm, welcoming tea room. The menu in the **Old Station Tea Rooms** ranges from a toasted sandwich to a Sunday roast, plus a delicious assortment of puddings, cakes and scones. Muddy boots are no problem here – there is an outside counter service and lots of picnic tables. Open April-September, Tuesday-Sunday, 10.00am-5.30pm. October-1 January & March,Tuesday-Sunday until 5.00pm. January/February, weekends until 5.00pm. Tel: 01425 402 468.

Distance: 5 ¾ miles.

How to get there: From Lyndhurst take the A35 Christchurch road for 7 miles to Holmsley. Immediately beyond the Holmsley sign turn left towards Burley. Turn right at the junction towards Sway. After one mile turn right to the car park.

Public Transport: Bus service: Wilts & Dorset.

Start: GR 251997. Wootton Bridge car park (free). If arriving by bus, start at paragraph 7.

Maps: Landranger 195; Outdoor Leisure 22.

---

1. From the car park turn left along the road to a junction. Go straight across the junction to a gently rising, wide grassy track which curves right.

    The tall tower in the distance, on the right, is Sway Tower, or Peterson's Folly. Mr Peterson, a retired Indian judge, built it in 1879, as an experiment in the usefulness of pre-cast concrete and as a means of providing local employment. No scaffolding was used: the concrete, cast in wooden frames, being hauled up by a crane inside the building. The tower is now a private house.

Wilverley Inclosure

2.   At the top of the track cross the drives to Wilverley Lodge and Wilverley Cottage then follow a narrow path across heathland to Wilverley Inclosure car park. Cross the car park to the 'Wilverley Wander' signpost and go through a gate on the left, just behind the post. Continue along a gravel track until reaching a commemorative stone dating the periods of inclosure.

3.   Here turn right. After 80 metres turn left. On reaching a crossing path continue ahead for 90 metres to a fork. Turn right for 100 metres; leave the inclosure by a wooden gate and turn left along a gravel track.

This track was once part of a smugglers' route from Lymington. The Naked Man, a skeleton trunk of an ancient oak, owes its sad state to a bolt of lightning. It is claimed to be a tree from which highwaymen and smugglers were hung.

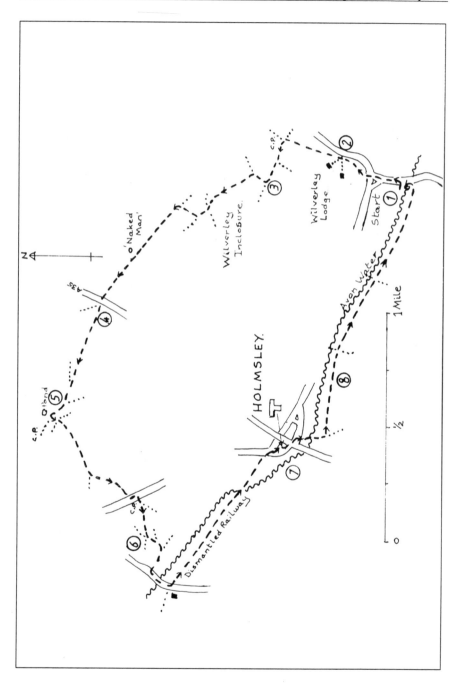

4. On reaching the A35 cross over to a stile. Keep forward on a grassy path through heather and scrub heathland; shortly pass an old milestone showing the distances to Ringwood, Lymington and Burley. As the path merges with a track from the left, it curves right and descends. Suddenly evidence of the old road is apparent, not only in the faded centre white line underfoot, more unusually there are a number of old traffic reflector signs bordering the road. Here find a narrow path between the two most prominent reflectors on the left, opposite a small pond on the right.

5. Descend for 12 metres between trees to emerge at a valley. Bear diagonally right to follow a narrow path along the right-hand side of the valley. At the bottom of the valley the path curves right, continues halfway round a clump of hawthorn on your left, then ascends through heather to a road. Turn left for 100 metres to Goatspen car park. Pass through the car park to a Forestry Commission bylaws sign. Immediately behind the sign, descend for 40 metres to a gravel track on the right. The track rises and dips to a crossing, at which point the views open out and electricity cables are seen on the left.

6. Turn left and gradually descend, soon passing under the electricity cables. The path now widens out a little, passes under a second set of cables and continues to a road. Turn left, cross two bridges and continue to a lone house on the right, Turn left through a barrier gate for a pleasant ¾ mile stroll along the dismantled railway track, through a diversity of beautiful woodland. Towards the end of the walk, on the right, is the only remaining section of the old station platform. At the end of the platform cross a stile and a road to the tea room.

Holmsley Station was opened in 1847 to serve the market towns of Wimborne and Ringwood. Although, for most of its life it was a quiet, picturesque New Forest station serving the local community, it did have some moments of glory. One of the station's first visitors was Prince Edward, who alighted there with Lillie Langtry, to be taken on by carriage to Bournemouth. Robert Louis Stevenson featured the station in his novel, *The Wrong Box*. During the Second World War, an aerodrome was built nearby. For four hectic years the station was used by hundreds of airmen; vast amounts of goods were handled and the war department had to build a special siding at the station in which to store ammunition. The station's last famous passenger was probably General Eisenhower, when he visited Holmsley Aerodrome in May 1944, to supervise preparations for the D-Day landings. During the 1950s, in addition to the normal service, special 'Sunday rambler' trains were provided for the discerning hiker. Inevitably, the increase of bus services and car ownership caused a gradual decline in the need for trains. Sadly, on 4th May 1964, the station fell to the 'Beeching Axe'.

7. From the tea room turn left to the junction with the A35. Cross over to the 40-mph zone sign. Eight metres beyond the sign (opposite a car park) turn right to cross a stile into a field. Cross ahead to a footbridge. Over the bridge turn left to walk through the beautiful lush meadow bordering Avon Water. Whilst crossing the meadow bear gradually left towards the river, so that, on entering the wood ahead, you meet the riverside path.

8. The route now follows the river through the wood back to the car park. Although the path disappears from time to time, if you stay within sight of the river you won't go wrong. Whilst the wood can be quite muddy after rain, it's a lovely walk: apart from the many wild flowers growing in the boggy areas, further interest is added by the occasional necessity to jump over small tributaries and duck under or climb over fallen trees. The path ends at a picnic area and the car park.

17. Burley & Whitten Pond

Route: A lovely walk on dry sandy tracks across open, gently undulating, heathland. The heather and gorse-covered heaths provide habitat for a rich diversity of birdlife; ponds passed *en route* are popular watering holes for the New Forest ponies.

Tea shop: **Manor Farm Tea Rooms** is a delightful 16th century thatched cottage. A tea room since 1904, it is the ideal place for a special treat. The varied menu includes light lunches, delicious home-made puddings and a tempting assortment of home-made cakes and scones. A full roast is served on Sundays. There is an attractive gift shop which also sells locally made jams, chutneys and mustards – to its own recipes. There is a small, attractive garden. It is open 10.00am-5.00pm but closed Monday morning in summer and all day Monday in winter. Tel: 01425 402218.

Distance: 5 miles.

How to get there: Burley is 5 miles southeast of Ringwood, signposted from Picket Post on the A31.

Public Transport: Bus Service: Wilts & Dorset.

Start: GR 211031. Village car park (free) at the rear of the Queen's Head Hotel.

Maps: Landranger 195; Outdoor Leisure 22.

Burley is a small, busy village, popular with tourists. It has quaint gift shops, thatched cottages, ponies and donkeys wandering freely along its streets under Commoners' rights; and a history of smugglers, witches and dragons! Legend states that nearby Burley Beacon was the home of a terrifying dragon, killed in battle by a brave knight, Sir Morris de Berkley. The 16th century Queen's Head Hotel has a long history of smuggling. Some years ago a secret cellar was discovered – it yielded a cache of bottles, coins and pistols. In the 1950s, Burley was the home of a White Witch, Sybil Leek. She was often seen walking through the village, in her long black cloak, carrying a pet jackdaw on her shoulder. Eventually local disapproval forced her to leave and she moved to America. It is believed, by

Witchcraft shop named by Sybil Leek

some, that an active witches' coven still exists in Burley. The village has a number of fascinating witchcraft gift shops. One of them, 'A Witches Coven', was named by Sybil Leek herself.

1. Leave the car park by the entrance on the left of the public toilets; turn right to the road junction. Turn left and climb up the road as far as a 'school' sign. Immediately beyond the sign cross over, pass through small barrier posts and bear left through a wooded area to a junction of paths and a sign for Moorhill House Hotel. Cross straight ahead to a path which bears slightly left; within a few metres, pass public toilets on the left.

2. Continue ahead at a crossing to enjoy a long straight walk across Turf Hill – spacious, open undulating heathland of heather and gorse, with far-reaching views on the right. On passing Burley Golf Course on your left, the view to the left also opens out. The track eventually descends, under electricity cables, to a footbridge over Avon Water. From the bridge, a gentle ascent leads to the ruins of Greenberry Bridge. (Until the late 1980s it was still possible to use this bridge, but by 1995 it had become unsafe and

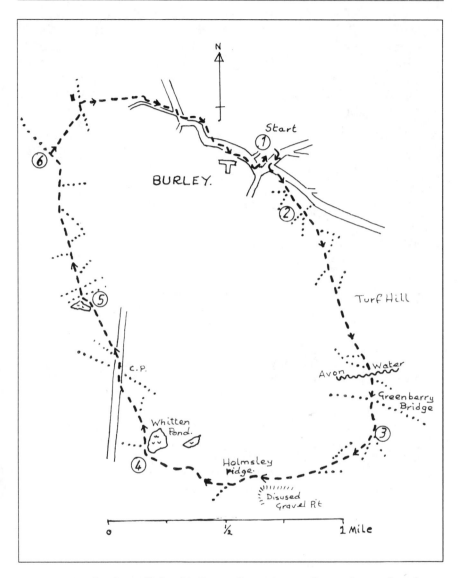

was partly demolished.) Cross the ruins and continue ahead until reaching a fork.

3. Take the right fork: in 12 metres, where there appears to be a left fork, continue ahead. This area of heather dominated heath is

Holmsley Ridge. The path soon widens out to a more established path; keep ahead as it merges with a path from the left. Shortly pass a gravel pit on the left. At the end of the quarry the track becomes very wide – almost road-like with 'islands' of heather down the middle. Where the track divides and forks left, keep ahead. In 200 metres gradually descend to Whitten Pond.

This is a delightful, peaceful spot – a little marshy at times which possibly explains why so few people frequent it – but their loss is our gain. It's perhaps prettiest in April when the surrounding gorse is in bloom or in summer when the waterlillies are out and a complete picture when ponies come down to drink at the water edge.

4. Walk round the pond to the noticeboard; ignore the path directly opposite the noticeboard and continue ahead. Keep left at a fork to reach the road. Turn right, crossing the dismantled railway, to the white-painted posts at an old bridge over a dried-up stream. Here cross over, bear right immediately behind the posts, pass under electricity cables in 120 metres and continue on.

5. As a pond is passed on your left, continue ahead. Keep ahead at a crossing. As this undulating track is traversed, a house can be seen over to the right set in the trees. On entering a slightly wooded area, cross two gravel footbridges within 50 metres. Keep ahead as the track merges with a path from the right: at this point in the far distance on the right a white house can be seen. When the track makes a short steep dip, ignore a grassy path on the right and continue ahead for almost ¼ mile to a very narrow, but obvious, path leading up to a hanger.

6. Turn right along the path, first walking through heather then gently ascending through bracken and the hanger to a wide gravel track. Turn left for 70 metres to a stile on your right. Over the stile, keep to the path as it meanders through woodland to a wooden gate on your right. From here descend between fencing to a road. Turn right then cross to the 'Village Centre' sign and follow the footpath as it skirts the road back to the village. Turn left along the main road to the tea shops. Turn through The Mall to return to the car park.

18. Acres Down and Holidays Hill Inclosure

Route: A varied, undulating walk across open heathland, through majestic woodland and quiet glades. The views from Acres Down are quite spectacular. The walk is perhaps best in early spring to enjoy the young foliage, or in autumn for the colours. Parts of the heathland are very wet in winter. As some of the paths are not too well-defined, an OS map and a compass are advisable.

Tea shop: **Acres Down Farm** serves cream teas only, but don't worry – this is one strictly for the self-indulgent, who wouldn't want it any other way. Delicious home-made scones, a choice of jams and a mountain of rich fresh cream are followed by a selection of mouth-watering home-made cakes – be warned, the choice is exceedingly difficult. Tea can be enjoyed either in the conservatory – an extension to the ever-open doors of Mr & Mrs Cooper's sitting room – or in their interesting plant-filled garden. It is open daily: April-September, 10.00am-6.00pm. Tel: 01703 813 693.

Distance: 6 ¾ miles.

How to get there: From Lyndhurst take the A35 towards Christchurch and follow signs to Emery Down. 1 ½ miles beyond the village turn left at a minor crossroad (the right turn is signposted 'Newtown'). Cross a ford, pass Acres Down Farm on the right and continue for 100 metres to the car park.

Public Transport: Bus service: Wilts & Dorset.

Start: GR 267097. Acres Down car park (free). If arriving by bus, start the walk at paragraph 6.

Maps: Landranger 195 & 196; Outdoor Leisure 22.

1. The walk starts from the rear of the car park. Ignore a path on the far left, head uphill and follow the track on the left of three tracks to a junction. Turn left, alongside birch on your right, for 40 metres to a narrow, deep gully and carefully drop down to a track. Continue straight across the open heathland. Shortly pass

through a small planting of mainly pine and birch and continue
for 100 metres to a fork. Fork right, climb gently for 60 metres
then fork right again.

The Portuguese Fireplace

2. The path gradually curves left, then curves right and gently descends, with scrub on the left. Continue between mainly holly and birch and shortly bear left into woodland. The path meanders through the wood in a southerly direction to a forest gate.

3. Pass through the gate and keep ahead for 175 metres to a broad, gravel, crossing track. Turn left along the track. Pass through a pair of gates and soon cross a footbridge over Highland Water – a pretty, tranquil spot, ideal for a rest stop. Reach Millyford Bridge car park and walk through to the road. Turn right for 200 metres to the Portuguese Fireplace.

    The flint fireplace marks the site of the camp occupied by a Portuguese Army Unit during the First World War. The unit was brought in to assist the depleted local labour force, which included The Women's Forestry Corps, in producing timber for the trenches in France and for pit-props for British coal mines.

4. Take a path immediately behind the information sign and walk parallel to the road until reaching a wooden gate on the left. Pass through the gate into Holidays Hill Inclosure and continue along the track. At a fork, take the left path and gradually ascend through a managed conifer plantation, where the heights of the trees range from one metre to a majestic thirty metres (about 100ft). The track leads to the car park for the Reptiliary.

    The Reptiliary is a breeding reserve for endangered species of reptiles and amphibians. It is surprisingly interesting – even for those of us who are not naturally snake lovers. Specially constructed enclosures allow amazing views of the sand lizard, a great variety of snakes, the natterjack toad and the European tree frog! Most of these creatures are eventually released into specially prepared sites in the New Forest. The reserve is open from Easter to October. Entrance is free to walkers passing through.

5. Leave the Reptiliary by the vehicular access gate. From the gate turn immediately acute right at the first of a number of barrier posts (opposite the 'cottage car park' sign) and continue parallel to the inclosure fence line. Soon cross a gravel footbridge and continue ahead for 35 metres to a fork. Fork left along a grassy path through woodland. Pass through a gate into Knightwood

Inclosure: the conifer, beech and oak here are some of the oldest and most magnificent trees in the forest. Continue ahead for 65 metres to a crossing path. Turn left, cross a stream and continue ahead. The path shortly curves left to Knightwood Oak car park. Turn left and follow the sign to the Knightwood Oak.

Monarch's Grove is a group of eighteen oaks planted around The Knightwood Oak, the most famous tree in the New Forest. The Oak is pollarded: an old custom and no longer practised in the New Forest. With a girth of 6.4 metres (21ft), it has the largest girth of all the oaks in the forest and at over 400 years old, it is also one of the oldest. In April 1979, the Queen and the Duke of Edinburgh each planted an oak tree to commemorate their visit to the forest. Monarch's Grove was then planted nearby, to record visits of eighteen previous monarchs, from William I to Edward VII.

6. From the grove, cross first to the fenced oak planted by the Queen, then to that planted by the Duke. Continue past the Duke's tree for 16 metres then turn right along a broad avenue of beech. Leave the inclosure through a gate to the open heathland. Cross the heath diagonally right to a gate at a road. Do not go through the gate, turn left for 40 metres to a footbridge, then continue parallel to the road to reach Warwickslade car park.

7. Cross the car park and leave it on the right of a barrier gate. Bear slightly right to join a grassy path between silver birch. The path, bordered by the birch, crosses the heath and continues through mixed woodland. Reach a gravel road, cross directly over and continue ahead. In 20 metres cross a bridge over Highland Water then climb for about 300 metres to a crossing path, with an island of trees in the middle. Continue ahead, now descending. Keep ahead at a crossing and continue to a long brick wall.

8. On reaching the wall, turn left. Walk initially parallel to it, then continue through the woodland. After $\frac{1}{4}$ mile cross a small stream. (Here, on the right, the woodland is a little more sparse and the open heathland more visible.) From the stream, climb between mainly holly trees to a crossing path.

9. Turn left. The path rises and falls (twice) then levels out to reach

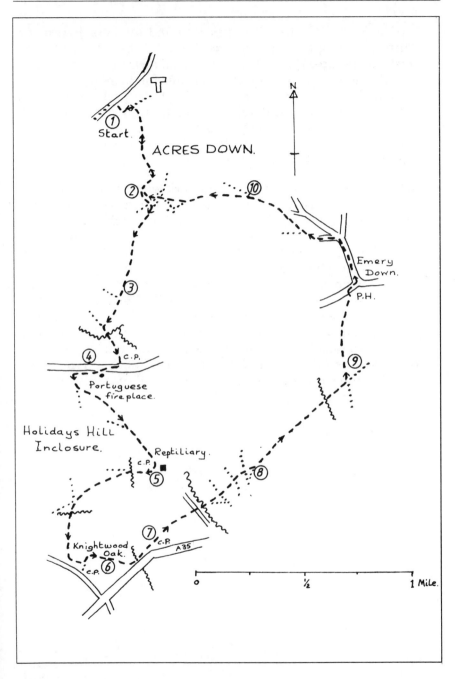

a road. Turn right to a road junction and the New Forest Inn. Turn left along the road to pass through Emery Down – don't miss the picture-postcard cottage tucked away on the right. Pass a road junction on the right and continue for 35 metres. Turn left on a track to a parking area. Pass through the parking area, with cottages on the right and follow the path through woodland. On reaching a fork, take the right-hand path to join a gravel road. Turn left along the road. Pass through a barrier gate onto a track which skirts woodland then downland.

10. Where the track curves to the right, fork left to climb to the summit of Acres Down. On reaching a fork, take the right-hand path and continue the now almost imperceptible climb to the summit. Enjoy the magnificent views southwards to Sway tower (see walk 16) and beyond to the downs on the Isle of Wight. The path soon merges with a path from the left. Here, turn right for 70 metres to a wide crossing path. Cross directly over to a narrow path and in 14 metres cross another wide path. The path gently descends and becomes more prominent: it sweeps right and joins, from the left, a path taken earlier in the walk. From this point the route is retraced. Continue ahead, pass through the pine and birch planting and climb the gully. Turn left then right to descend to the car park. The teashop, you will recall, is two minutes walk away.

19. Minstead and The Rufus Stone

Route: This is a lovely walk, full of interest. The New Forest is a delight at any season and there is always something to catch the eye in Furzey Gardens. Although the walking is easy, with only slight undulations, the paths through the Forest at instructions 1 & 3 are not particularly well-defined; an OS map and a compass are advisable.

Tea shop: **Honeypot Tea Room** is a delightful extension to Honeysuckle Cottage, a licensed restaurant. In the cottage garden, tables are attractively arranged, garden party style, under gazebos and large parasols. A varied menu includes home-made hot meals and delicious clotted cream teas. Open daily: April-September, 10.00am-5.30pm. October-March ,Wednesday-Sunday, 11.00am-3.30pm. Tel: 01703 813 122.

Distance: 5 miles.

How to get there: From the A336 Cadman road, follow the A337 towards Lyndhurst for ¾ mile. Turn right towards Minstead, do not fork left to the village; keep ahead for ½ mile to Hazel Hill car park.

Public Transport: Bus services: Both Wilts & Dorset and Solent Blue Line stop in Minstead.

Start: GR 289117. Hazel Hill car park (free). If arriving by bus, start at paragraph 8.

Maps: Landranger 195; Outdoor Leisure 22.

1. From the car park turn left along the road. As the road sweeps left, keep ahead along a track signed 'Suter's Cottage'. Just before reaching the cottage turn right through a Forestry Commission barrier gate, keep ahead, passing immediately to the right of a thick, gnarled old oak. Continue ahead in a westerly direction through the forest – this path appears to be used more by horse-riders than walkers and is not particularly well-defined, so take care not to wander off route. After ¾ mile a point is reached where a garden is clearly visible on the left, with the house just showing through the trees. Here continue ahead to a lane.

2. Turn right along the lane. Just before reaching the road (A31) take a path on the right of a cattle grid. The path leads down to, and under, the motorway. From the tunnel, continue along the path to a drive and then turn right.

3. Twenty-five metres before reaching a gate across the drive, turn right into the forest: the path meanders in a northerly direction for 1/3 mile to a clearing. Cross the clearing to Grey's Farmhouse and turn right along the drive. Immediately beyond Langley Cottage, turn left at 'Woodpeckers' onto a broad grassy path. At the end of the houses the path becomes a forest track skirting the left of the forest: follow it through to a lane. Keep ahead to a junction.

4. Turn left along a road and shortly pass the Sir Walter Tyrrell public house. Take a track at the end of the pub car park. In quick succession go through two low barrier gates then turn right to a car park and the road. Cross over to the Rufus Stone.

   The present Rufus Stone was erected in 1841. It marks the spot where an oak tree stood, from which, on 2 August 1100, an arrow shot by Sir Walter Tyrrell at a stag, glanced and hit King William II (Rufus) causing his immediate death. Rufus was then put in a cart and 'drawn from hence to Winchester, where he is buried in the Cathedral Church of that City'.

5. With your back to that side of the stone referring to the journey to Winchester, go forward, south west, across the common. As the common opens out, the path bears slightly left and gently ascends to a crossing path. Eighty metres beyond the crossing, the path curves left. (There is an overflow pipe, set in concrete, just to the right.) The path soon merges with a track from the right; it leads back under the motorway and continues to a junction.

6. Turn left along a wide gravel track. Keep right at a fork, immediately passing Yew Tree Cottage (note the small window beautifully inscribed with the house name). The track passes houses then merges with a drive from the left. Twenty-five metres beyond the drive, fork left along a broad forest track. On leaving the forest keep ahead along a lane, soon passing Furzey Gardens on the right.

   Furzey Gardens comprise eight acres of delightful landscape with exten-

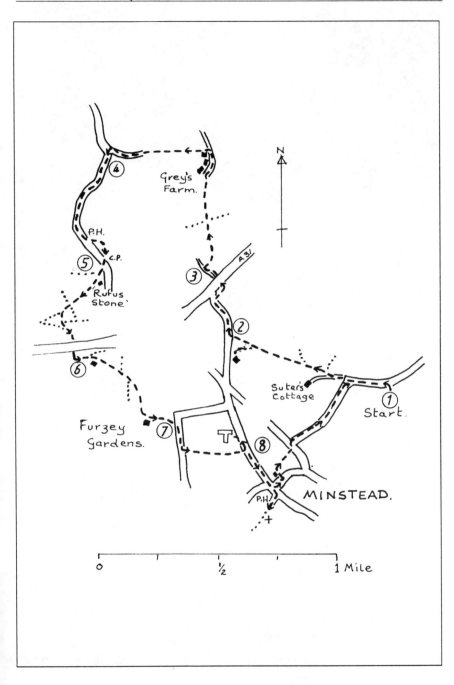

Furzey Gardens

sive views over the New Forest and towards the Isle of Wight. It has a water garden and, in their seasons, magnificent banks of azaleas and rhododendrons, heathers, the strange bottle brush tree and flaming Chilean Fire trees. The tiny brick and timber cottage at the entrance, still with its original fireback and bread oven, is a thought-provoking example of 16th century primitive life. For further information, tel: 01703 812 464.

7. At the end of the gardens turn right then right again along a road. After 200 metres, turn left over a stile into a field. Keeping the hedgerow on your left, cross two fields to a road. Turn left for 140 metres to **Honeypot Tea Room**.

Set in undulating countryside, with clusters of thatched cottages, Minstead is one of the New Forest's quieter, more peaceful villages. It has a small village green, around which are the post office-cum-general store, an inn and the parish church.

The unusually named Trusty Servant Inn has a sign depicting a man with a pig's snout, the ears of an ass and the feet of a stag: a rhyme underneath explains its reasoning. The church, one of only two in the Forest mentioned in the Domesday Book, has a welcoming, homely atmosphere. Uniquely, it has a three decker pulpit, two galleries, and three Georgian 'Parlour Pews'. The pews, erected for local gentry, had their own entrance, furnishings, fireplace and chimney. One of the pews still has its fireplace and comfortable chairs. Sir Arthur Conan Doyle, who lived for a time in the parish, is buried in the churchyard.

8. From the tea room turn right to walk down to the village. Turn right at the Trusty Servant Inn to visit the church. Return to the main road, turn left then immediately right at picturesque Dunbridge Cottage. Turn left at Manor Farm cottage. Pass through a kissing-gate and continue along a narrow path, sheltered in summertime under a welcome tree canopy, to a road. Turn left to a junction. Turn right along Seaman's Lane for ¾ mile to the car park.

20. Fordingbridge &
The Avon Valley Path

Route: A diversity of terrain with fields, farmtracks, water meadows and
                      Blissford Common. A beautiful walk with superb views at many stages.

Tea shop: **Ivy Cottage**, a charming, part 16th century building, may not have the
                      appearance of a rambler's tea shop, but the owners offer a warm
                      welcome to all-comers. The cosy dining room has open timber beams
                      and an inglenook fireplace. A varied menu offers breakfast, light
                      lunches and delicious home-made cakes and scones. There is a very
                      pretty rear garden. A word of warning for muddy boot days: don't
                      remove them until you've visited the loo – it's accessed via the garden!
                      Open all year, except Christmas, Tuesday-Saturday, 8.00am-5.00pm.
                      Sunday, 1.00pm-5.00pm. Tel: 01425 654 515.

Distance: 6½ miles.

How to get there: Fordingbridge is on the A338, 6 miles north of Ringwood.

Public Transport: Bus services: Wilts & Dorset.

Start: GR 148143. Town car park (free), drive through to long stay area.

Maps: Landranger 195; Outdoor Leisure 22.

1. From the car park, pass through 'The Hundred' (a passage next to
    the mini-market). Cross over into Bridge Street and cross the
    River Avon.

    Before turning left, it's well worth going into the recreation ground on the
    right, for a lovely view of the river and the bridge. In Saxon times, Fording-
    bridge was a milling community. For many years there was just a ford at
    this important crossing point of the Avon. The impressive seven-arched
    bridge was built in the 14th century and is now designated an ancient
    monument. Today, apart from St Mary's Church on the south of the
    town, the bridge is all that remains of the town's medieval history.
    Tucked away in the trees at the side of the bridge, is a life-size bronze of
    Augustus John: a 'Bohemian giant of an artist' whose favourite themes

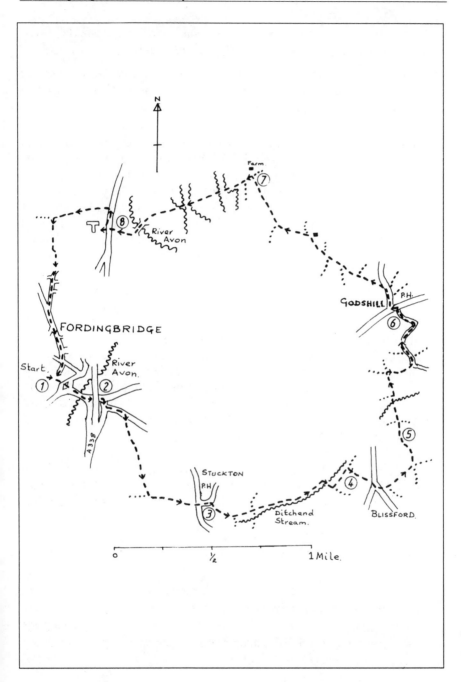

were gypsies, fishing folk and wild beautiful women. Augustus John lived in Fordingbridge, with his large family, from 1927 until his death in 1961.

Currently, excavations in the town have uncovered evidence of a riverside tannery and pottery from the 13th century, as well as foundations of a building which may also be 13th century.

2. Turn left and pass under a road bridge. Turn right towards Stuckton then immediately left along a minor road. Reach Fordingbridge Bowling Club and turn right over a stile. Keep left of a barn to a further stile. Follow a left-hand boundary across three fields. In a fourth field keep a copse on your right. Go straight across a fifth field then bear slightly left in a sixth field towards the right of a hedge. Turn left within the field to a gate and stile. Continue ahead along a broad grassy path.

3. On reaching Stuckton Road, cross over to a minor road. After 80 metres, turn right onto a broad gravel track. In 20 metres cross a stile on the left and continue along a track which has a small stream running alongside and may be rather muddy after rain. On reaching a crossing path with three stiles, cross the stile immediately ahead. Following the line of Ditchend Brook, cross four fields via stiles and one footbridge. Leave the fourth field over two footbridges on the right. Follow a left-hand field boundary to a further footbridge. Turn left over the bridge and continue alongside a copse to a memorial fingerpost.

4. Here, turn right towards Blissford; ascend to a gate and keep ahead to a road. Cross over into Abbotswell Road. After 30 metres turn left through a large metal gate. After 40 metres turn left over a stile. Follow a left-hand field boundary up to a stile into Blissford Common. Continue ahead on a grassy path. After 200 metres, at a crossing path, turn left to gently ascend Blissford Hill.

Pause at the summit to soak up the fantastic view of the open heathland and the surrounding hills, marvellous when the gorse is out, superb when the heather is in flower and the ideal spot to sit and plan a ridge walk for another day. The Common and surrounding hills form part of the western edge of the New Forest.

5. Keep ahead across the summit, then descend to a gravel track. Bear left along the track towards a metal gate and stile. Pass through the gate and continue along a track. Cross Ditchend Brook, turn right, then left alongside a riding school. Cross a stile and turn right to a footbridge and stile. Follow a left-hand field boundary uphill to a stile on the left of an electricity pole. Over the stile, a track, with houses either side, leads to a lane. Turn left along the lane to reach Godshill. (The lane skirts Godshill Common, a lovely common with fine views – you could go onto and meander along it, but keep parallel to the lane.)

6. Cross to the Fighting Cocks public house and turn right towards Wood Green. After 150 metres turn left along a footpath. Cross a stile into a field. Follow a left-hand boundary to two stiles. Over the stiles follow a right-hand boundary to a stile and a grassy track. The track leads to a lone house. Here turn left along a broad track. The track skirts a wood then descends between fields, with excellent views across the Avon valley. At the bottom of the track turn left onto the Avon Valley Path (AVP).

The Avon Valley Path is a 34-mile walk from Salisbury to Christchurch. Much of the route goes through areas spared the ravages of modern agriculture and provides opportunity to discover a rich variety of wildlife. In their seasons, dog roses, blackberries and an abundance of wildflowers grow unrestrained in hedgerows of hornbeam, beech and hazel. Flourishing in the water meadows are kingcups, meadow sweet, tubular water-dropwort and the delicately flowered water-aven. The Avon valley is an important site for many species of birds. Lapwing, redshank, snipe, golden plover and a variety of buntings and warblers are all there to be found – with luck you may even spot the elusive kingfisher. The walk would be lovely for a 'long weekend', especially if contemplating a first long distance walk.

7. The track passes between fields and through water meadows, via a series of footbridges. Finally, the Avon itself is crossed via an elegant pedestrian suspension bridge, the only one of its kind in Hampshire. Turn right and pass through a farmyard to reach a road. Cross over to the tea shop.

8. Refreshed and with your back to the tea shop, turn left along the

road. Reach Burgate Farm and turn left to follow the Avon Valley Path again. The track passes the farm and continues alongside a sports field. Turn left at a corner of the field (AVP) and continue to a road. Turn right. On reaching a junction, turn left along Whitsbury Road. At the end of the road, cross into The Bartons to return to the car park.

Suspension bridge over the River Avon

21. Breamore Manor & Rockbourne

Route: Beautiful rolling downland with marvellous views; superb, undulating woods; a picturesque thatched village and a splendid Elizabethan manor – this is one of our favourite rambles. Perhaps most enjoyable in spring for the bluebells or autumn for the colour.

Tea shop: **Breamore Manor** tea shop is a cosy, weather-boarded chalet with an attractive trellis-enclosed patio. The service is friendly and the menu offers light lunches and home-made cakes and scones. It is open from 12noon – 6.00pm Sunday, Tuesday & Wednesday in April, plus Saturday & Thursday from May to July, and every day in August. Tel: 01725 512 468.

Distance: 7 miles.

How to get there: Breamore is on the A338, 3 miles north of Fordingbridge. The Manor House is signposted.

Public Transport: Bus service: Skylark Motor Services.

Start: GR 151187. Breamore Manor House car park (free).

Maps: Landranger 184; Outdoor Leisure 22; Pathfinder 1262 SU 02/12.

Breamore Manor House is an elegant, gabled, Elizabethan manor set in beautiful parkland, overlooking the Avon Valley. The manor was devastated by fire in 1856; with the exception of the original front façade, the building is a skilful restoration. In the 18th century, the manor was bought by Sir Edward Hulse, Court Physician to Queen Anne, King George I and George II. Today it is still the Hulse's family home. The manor has a Country Museum in the old stables; both are open to the public from spring to autumn. Visitors will see two splendid original fireplaces, as well as fine paintings, period furniture and much of historical interest. The museum provides a fascinating insight into village life of past times. There is a fine collection of carriages and steam-powered machinery and an award-winning modern brick maze. For further information, tel: 01725 512 468.

1. Walk through the courtyard, turn right then left through the 'lion guarded' gates of Breamore Manor for a pleasant stroll through the grounds: take time to admire the magnificent cedars, beech

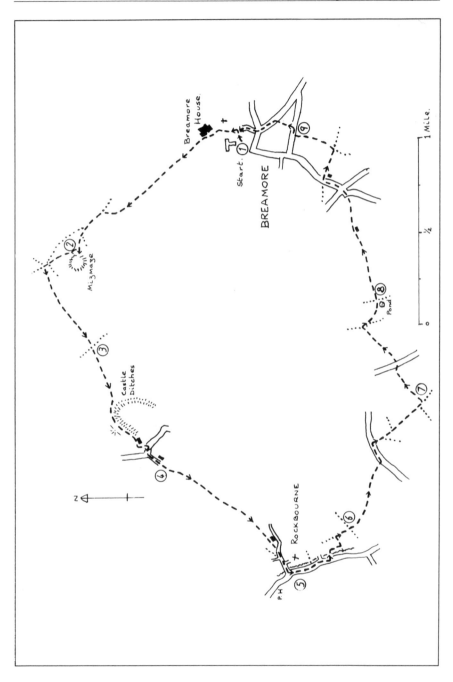

The Mizmaze

and oak. Pass the Manor House, noting the disused chapel standing forlornly in the trees, and steadily ascend through Breamore Wood – an ancient wood of beech, oak, sweet chestnut and yew. The track levels out at a junction of private drives and soon descends to open fields, with expansive views across the downland. Keep left at a junction. Bear left at a fork and turn immediately right uphill to the mizmaze – tread carefully, harebells and field scabious flower prolifically here.

High on the chalk down, enclosed by a grove of yew, is the mysterious, prehistoric Breamore Mizmaze. Nearly 28 metres wide, its grassy path curves symmetrically to a central mound. Its origin and use is unknown but it is thought the maze may have been traversed by monks, on their knees, as an act of penance.

2. Return to the field, turn left at the signboard and enjoy the extensive views eastwards across the Avon Valley whilst descending gradually on an angle. At the bottom of the field, the path merges with a path from the right, turn left. In 20 metres, ignore a stile on the left and continue to a second stile. Turn left over the stile and follow a left-hand boundary down the field – take time to enjoy

the magnificent views across Breamore Down. Continue ahead through a wood of ancient yew and beech. From the wood keep ahead on a grassy path, descending eventually to a stile and a crossing track.

3. Cross the track for a long, steady climb alongside a wooden fence. At the summit are Whitsbury Castle Ditches, the site of an ancient hill fort and now sadly hidden behind impenetrable trees. Northwards are magnificent views to Salisbury Plain. On a clear day, the tall, slender steeple of the Cathedral is visible. Descend round the fort to Whitsbury Manor racing stables. Pass a beautiful thatched tithe barn and continue through the stables to a road. Turn right along the road. Turn left at the junction to reach a wooden gate just ahead.

4. Pass through the gate to walk along a grassy avenue of fine beech trees. Pass through two gates in quick succession and descend, first between beech, chestnut and oak on the left and conifer on the right, then through a magnificent grove of beech and horse chestnut. Pass through two metal gates, again in quick succession and go straight across a long field to a farm track. Keep ahead to the farm and follow waymarks to a lane and continue to a road.

   It's worth turning off the lane to see the elegant, part medieval manor house and to visit the beautifully positioned Norman church. The church's many features include monuments to the Coote family. Advice from General Sir Eyre Coote enabled Clive (of India) to achieve victory in a decisive battle at Plassey in 1757. The menfolk of the Coote family were all bald: to be 'as bald as a coote' is said to refer to the family and not the water-bird!

   Set in beautiful rolling countryside, over-looked by its church and manor house, Rockbourne is a delight. Its winding road is bordered with a cress-filled chalk stream, over which tiny bridges give access to picturesque thatched cottages. Along the road, to the right, are a few pretty cottages of cruck construction and the 16th century Rose & Thistle public house.

5. Turn left to walk through the village. Pass a house, 'Abbot's Acre', and turn left over a footbridge towards Minty's Hill. Ascend to some cream-painted houses and a green. Turn right

along the lower edge of the green and the following two gardens. Cross a stile and turn immediately left alongside a field boundary. Pass through a metal gate and turn right onto a narrow track.

6. Keep ahead at a crossing and soon reach a large open field, with excellent views of the downs. The monument in the far distance is a memorial to General Coote. Cross the field, skirt a copse on your left, and continue to a stile. Turn left along a lane and climb for 160 metres to a gravel track. Turn right to ascend through woodland and soon ignore an ascending track on the right. On leaving the wood continue ahead between fields.

7. Reach a wood and turn left into it. The path meanders along the fringe of the wood, with a breathtaking display of bluebells in springtime. On reaching a road, cross diagonally right into another wood. Ascend to a waymarked junction. Turn right; keep ahead at the next waymarked post and follow waymarkers (on the trees) through the wood.

8. Cross a track and bear very slightly left across a field to a stile into a wood. The path meanders through the wood to a more open, grassy area. Cross this, keeping to the right, to reach a track between trees. Soon cross a stile and pass a house on the right. At the road continue ahead towards Breamore, climbing for 200 metres to two cottages. Here, turn right, keep to a right-hand field boundary until it turns right, then go straight across the field. Cross a stile and turn immediately left alongside a field boundary. Cross another stile and follow a grassy path to a road.

9. Turn right for 30 metres to a footpath on the left, leading into a field. Bear left across the field to a signpost in the hedge, then drop down to the road. Turn left to a junction. Cross over and walk down a drive to Breamore Church; turn left to the tea room.

Picturesquely situated, surrounded by beautiful trees, Breamore Church is a gem. The finest example of a Saxon church in Hampshire, it has much to delight the eye. In the south porch is a striking sculpture of the Crucifixion. Its most remarkable antiquity is an Anglo-Saxon inscription on the arch of the south transept. It translates 'Here the Covenant becomes manifest to thee.' It is thought to date from the latter part of the reign of Ethelred II (979-1016).

22. The Water Ways of Romsey

Route: A pleasant, easy route with fieldpaths, undulating woodland, the
                    riverside, a towpath and a small amount of road-walking. It is probably
                    most enjoyed in dry conditions – after prolonged rainfall the fields at
                    the beginning tend to be waterlogged. The name Romsey means
                    'island in the marshes'!

Tea shop: Plenty of opportunity to indulge on this walk! Halfway along the route is
                    the **World of Water Tea Room**. Being part of a garden centre, one
                    needn't feel out of place in (clean) boots here. The menu offers
                    home-made light meals and cakes. Open daily: mid-March to the end
                    of October,9.00am-4.30pm. Tel: 01794 515 923.

                    La Café Boulangerie is a pretty French café in the Market Square.
                    Outside seating enables one to sit and watch the world go by whilst
                    enjoying a baguette, a gateau or one of their seventeen varieties of
                    New Forest ice-cream. Open daily: 10.00am-9.00pm.
                    Tel: 01794 518 555.

                    Tilly's Tea Room is cosy and traditional with a pretty walled garden.
                    The menu offers an excellent array of home-made light meals, cakes
                    and scones. Open summer; Monday-Saturday, 8.00am-5.00pm.
                    Sunday, 10.00am-4.00pm. Winter until 4.30pm, closed Sundays.
                    Tel: 01794 512 351.

Distance: 6 miles.

How to get there: Romsey is at the junction of the A31 and B3057, 10 miles south west
                    of Winchester.

Public Transport: Bus service: Stagecoach Hampshire Bus, Solent Blue Line, Wilts &
                    Dorset. Trains: South West Trains.

Start: GR 355213. Love Lane car park (pay & display).

Maps: Landranger 185; Explorer 131; Pathfinder 1263 SU 22/32.

There is much to explore and delight in Romsey: the Market Square
with its old coaching inns and Lord Palmerston's statue; Church
Court with its 18th century cottages and 13th century King John's
House; a house with original door and window surrounds – and

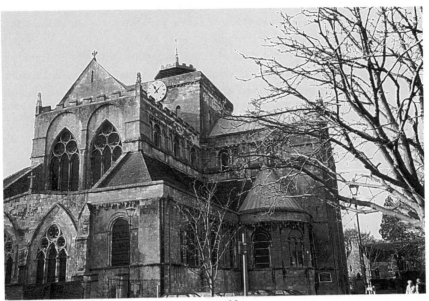

Romsey Abbey

medieval graffiti on its walls; the lovely river and backwaters, and the magnificent Romsey Abbey.

The history of Romsey is reflected in the growth of its majestic Abbey. A church (a wooden building) was established in Romsey in 907 by King Edward the Elder. Rebuilding, which began around 966 by Edward the Peaceful, continued throughout the centuries. For six hundred years, the Abbey was the home of Benedictine Nuns. During the Dissolution, many parts of the Abbey were destroyed, but the fabric remained. In 1554, it was saved from further destruction when the townspeople were able to purchase it for £100. The actual deed of purchase from Henry VIII, together with other Romsey documents and antiquities, is displayed in an ancient chest. The Abbey also contains some of the finest 12th and 13th century work to be found in England. It is a warm welcoming place, well worth visiting. On the external wall of the south transept is a superb 11th century carving of Christ, with the hand of God appearing from a cloud.

1. Leave the car park by the Town Centre exit, turn right into Love Lane (note **Tilly's Tea Room** on the corner). Continue along The Hundred into Corn Market Square.

Lord Palmerston, born in Romsey in 1784, was brought up at Broadlands. He entered politics late in life and for over thirty years was a dominant force in the Foreign Office. As Foreign Secretary he was famous for his aggressive, yet occasionally liberal policies. A reformer and a free trader, he believed Victorian England was the only true world power. He became Prime Minister, leading the Liberal coalition, in 1855 and again in 1859 until his death in 1865.

2. Keep left of Lord Palmerston's statue, pass under the archway of the Old Abbey and continue along The Meads, passing a side entrance to Romsey Abbey on your right. Cross the River Test and turn left into the Memorial Gardens.

    The gun in the Gardens was captured in Burma during the Second World War and donated to the town by Earl Mountbatten: the Earl is buried in the south transept of Romsey Abbey.

3. Keep to the right-hand path through the gardens and leave by a gate on the right just before reaching the public toilets. Turn left over a tributary of the Test and continue alongside houses on your left to soon cross the Test at Sadler's Mill. Immediately beyond the mill turn right between houses (Nos. 3 & 5); at the end of the garden turn right onto the Test Way. Follow the Way straight through the fields, crossing two footbridges. From the second footbridge veer left to the far corner of the field and cross a footbridge into Squabb Wood. Skirt the right side of the wood, cross a stile and footbridge over a small stream and continue deeper into the wood, soon crossing a second footbridge. Immediately after a slight ascent, ignore a path on the left and continue along the Test Way, almost immediately crossing a footbridge.

4. On reaching a waymarked junction turn right (TW), and soon cross a footbridge into a clearing. Keep ahead through the clearing, gently ascending to the wood. Pass a waymarked seat – possibly the remains of a stile and skirt the right side of the wood. Cross a footbridge and continue ascending. Leave the wood by a wooden gate into a field.

5. Turn right, leaving the Test Way, continue alongside a large pig farm, gently ascending to the brow. Turn right along a way-

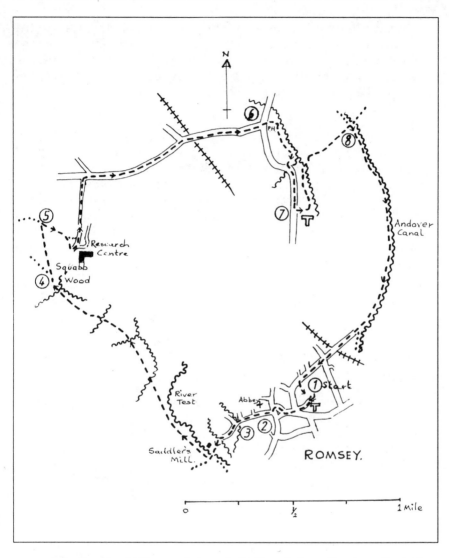

marked path. At the road, turn left, then left again at a sub station onto a gravelled track. On reaching a lane turn right: the lane twists and turns for about half a mile as it descends to a junction. Turn right, cross a railway bridge and continue for a third of a mile to The Duke's Head public house: this busy road also twists and turns – there is very little verge, so take great care.

6. Take the footpath on the left of the public house; at the end of the garden turn right along a grassy path. Turn right and follow the riverbank to the road. Turn left, cross the Test and continue along the road until reaching a garden centre and the **World of Water Tea Room**.

7. Turn left by the tea room. After 50 metres, turn left over a stile to follow the riverside path. Cross a footbridge and continue alongside the river. It now becomes necessary to watch for overhead electricity wires – you will probably spot them on the far side of the river first. Twelve metres beyond the wires take a narrow path on the right; if you look across the river you will see an electricity pole immediately opposite the path. Follow the path through light woodland, with a stream on your right. Cross a footbridge, then a concrete bridge and continue, now between two streams, until reaching a bridge over the Andover Canal.

This lovely canal walk, in total two miles long, is the only remaining part of the Andover to Redbridge Canal. Constructed in 1794, it went out of use in 1859 when superseded by the railway. Bordered with trees, shrubs and wild flowers, the canal provides an ideal habitat for a variety of water fowl including a family of swans. In summertime children with their canoes add colour and vibrancy to the peaceful scene.

8. Turn right along the towpath. Continue alongside the canal as the towpath changes to a lane. At a fork, turn right towards Romsey. At the junction, keep ahead into Station Road. Turn left into Orchard Lane to return to the car park.

23. Mottisfont & Spearywell Wood

Route: A pleasant walk through woods and fields to a charming Test Valley village. Perhaps most enjoyable during a dry spell – the fields around Lockerley can be a little marshy after rain. Those who wish to extend the walk a little may like to visit the famous Mottisfont Abbey Gardens – NT members, don't forget your cards!

Tea shop: **Mottisfont Post Office & Tea Room** is beautifully situated in the centre of the village. The menu includes light lunches and delicious home-made cakes and scones. There is a large attractive front garden. Open April-September, Tuesday-Sunday, 11.00am-5.30pm. Tel: 01794 340 243.

Distance: 6 miles.

How to get there: Mottisfont is off the A3057, 5½ miles north of Romsey. The car park is on the B3084, 1 mile north west of Mottisfont.

Public Transport: Bus services: Broughton & Mottisfont Village Bus. Trains: South Wales & West Railways.

Start: GR 316277. Spearywell Wood NT car park (free). If arriving by train start at paragraph 7.

Maps: Landranger 185; Explorer 131; Pathfinder 1263 SU22/32.

Spearywell Wood is a diverse mixture of conifer and broad-leaved trees and it provides habitat for a profusion of wildlife. Roe and Fallow deer roam freely in the woodland glades; buzzards fly high above the tree canopy. Butterflies to be discovered include the speckled wood and the rare silver-washed fritillary. In autumn, weird and wonderful fungi include the aptly named stinkhorn and the fairy-tale fly agaric mushroom.

1. Take the woodland path on the left of the 'National Trust Mottisfont Estate' sign. The path dips and rises as it meanders through the wood to a T-junction (immediately to the right of the junction is a short length of wooden fencing). Turn left along a gently ascending grassy path to a T-junction. Turn right to skirt the wood. At a junction of paths, with a two-way signpost, turn sharp right

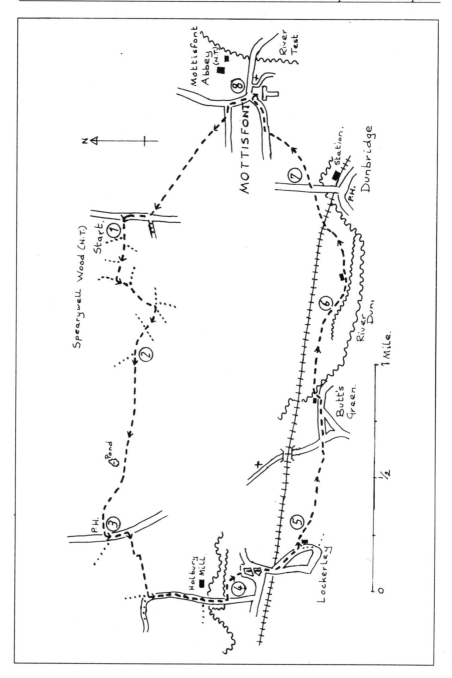

to descend deeper into the wood. Cross a footbridge and a track
and continue ahead. The path descends to a stile into a field.

2. Turn left alongside the field boundary and cross a further stile.
    Head slightly left towards a lone stile on the right of a series of
    clumps of trees, then continue towards a group of five oaks. Pass
    between the oaks and continue towards two oaks: behind them is
    a kissing-gate. Through the gate, bear left across a field towards a
    group of pine in the border of a small copse. (The handsome mel-
    low red-brick mansion over on the right is Lockerley Hall). Pass
    through a kissing-gate and continue through the copse, passing a
    pond on the right, to a stile. Cross the parkland to a stile ahead.
    Continue through a conifer plantation into a field. Head towards
    and pass through a cricket field. Pass by The Star Inn, to a road.

3. Turn left for 200 metres to a stile on the right into a field. Cross
    ahead to a footbridge. Over the bridge follow a right-hand field
    boundary, climbing to a track and a lane. Turn left. The lane de-
    scends past Holbury Mill, crosses the River Dun, then passes by
    Holbury Lakes. Just beyond the lakes, turn left over a stile into a
    meadow and follow a stream on your left to a stile. Continue
    along a fenced path to Lockerley village green.

4. Cross the full length of both the greens, bearing left to the road
    junction. Take the road ahead, which ascends to a railway bridge
    and a junction. Here fork left along Lockerley Common. Turn left
    at the last of the group of houses: this last house is comparatively
    large with ivy-clad walls. The path is on the left of the house,
    there is a signpost – behind a large bush! Pass through a gate at
    the end of the house into the garden, go past the greenhouses to a
    stile into a field and bear right to cross a further stile.

5. Follow a line of electricity cables down a field, heading towards a
    group of houses bordering the field. (The lovely church seen
    from the field is Lockerley parish church.) Keep right of the ca-
    bles to reach and cross a stile into a garden. Follow the right-
    hand hedge to a narrow path bordering the garden and leading to
    a road. Cross over and follow the Mottisfont road to the end of
    Butt's Green and a house 'Dunmead' just beyond. Turn left to a
    footbridge over the River Dun. Cross the bridge and turn immedi-

ately right over a stile into a field (this could be quite wet after rain). Cross diagonally towards two footbridges in the middle of the field, maintain the same direction to a further footbridge and a stile into a field.

6. Cross to the right of the first electricity pole and pass through an iron barrier into an area of scrub. Keep ahead through the scrub to emerge at a lone thatched cottage with two wooden gates just beyond. Pass through the gate on the right and follow a left-hand field boundary straight across two fields to a railway crossing. Cross with care and follow a track to a road.

7. Cross over to a stile into a field. Bear left, climbing to the right of a group of trees at the summit. Pass between the last two oaks and continue in the same direction towards a large lone oak at the field boundary. Follow a fenced path which borders the field, to a lane. Turn right to Mottisfont and the tea shop. Walk past the tea shop and round the corner to see the old part of the village.

Mottisfont village and Abbey is owned by the National Trust. Just two minutes walk from the post office, pretty thatched cottages and the intimate 12th century church with its shingle spire sit peacefully in wooded surroundings. It is said that this lovely church contains more 15th century glass than any other Hampshire church. Less than ¼ mile further along the country lane is Mottisfont Abbey.

Mottisfont was never designated an Abbey. It was a 12th century Priory, which at the time of the Dissolution, was converted into a large Tudor mansion. In the 1740s, it was transformed into a Georgian house. The medieval remains include an almost complete vaulted cellarium – the monks' storeroom. In 1938, Rex Whistler was engaged to decorate a drawing room in *trompe l'oeil*. False columns, pelmets and plasterwork are all painted in extravagant detail. A painted niche containing a smoking urn has a reality which is truly amazing. Hidden in a corner, a paint pot and brush wait for the painter's return – a poignant picture – Whistler did not return from the war.

The charm of Mottisfont is in its surroundings. Large expansive lawns sweep down to the River Test. Planted in the lawns are magnificent specimen trees: blue cedar, mulberry, oak and a gigantic plane tree, thought to be the largest in the country. It is these trees and the beau-

Mottisfont Abbey

tiful rose garden, planted in 1972 to conserve the early French roses, which attracts visitors from all over the world. The rose garden now contains over 350 varieties. In June and July it is a magical place, especially in the quiet of early evening. For opening hours and the best time to visit for the roses, tel: 01794 340 757.

8. Follow the road opposite the tea shop to a junction. Turn left into Bengers Lane. After 40 metres turn right over a stile into a large open field. Bear left across the field, passing between two oaks. Cross a footbridge into another large field and maintain the same direction, heading slightly right of an electrical pylon in the distance. Leave the field at its left-hand corner. Turn right along the road to return to the car park.

24. Longstock, Danebury Hill & Stockbridge

Route: The route climbs from Longstock to Danebury Hill; fields and tracks undulate and there is a small amount of road-walking. However, this is a superb walk and any effort expended is well rewarded. There are beautiful views at all stages and throughout spring and summer a riot of wild flowers flourish on Danebury Hill and amongst the hedgerows. Finally, in Longstock, one of the most beautiful reaches of the River Test is crossed.

Tea shop: From a large selection of eating places we chose **Lillie**, an attractive tea room and bakery. The owners Bernard & Ninya Van Galen are justly proud of their home-made soup and cakes; the 'filled' baguettes and croissants are, quite simply, a major understatement. The tea room is cosily furnished, but in summer most people prefer to be outside where they can 'duckwatch' from their seats on a bridge over the stream. Open summer, 9.30am-5.30pm. Winter; 9.30am-5.00pm. Closed in the last three weeks of January. Tel: 01264 810 754.

Distance: 7½ miles.

How to get there: From Stockbridge take the A30 towards Salisbury. Immediately on crossing the River Test, turn right for 1¼ miles to Longstock. Turn left into Church Road.

Public Transport: Bus service: Stagecoach Hampshire Bus.

Start: GR 359371. Roadside parking in Church Road, Longstock.

Maps: Landranger 185; Explorer 131; Pathfinder 1242 SU23/33.

1. From the car climb for about one mile along Church Road, a quiet country road used only by local residents, farmers, horse-riders – and hikers! The road soon becomes a rough track along which a pleasant easy ascent can be enjoyed. On reaching the summit (at two barns), there are fine views across the rolling downland. The track descends, with equally good views ahead, to a road junction. (At the junction take note that across the road is the track to which you return from Danebury Hillfort.)

2. Ignore the road curving right and take the road straight ahead – this is a busy road and care is needed, but it's still possible to enjoy the superb views on the right. At the 'Danebury Hillfort' sign, turn left to climb to the fort. Pass through a car park, with public toilets and continue to the trig. point. After taking your fill of the magnificent views of the surrounding countryside, follow the signs to the fort.

    Covering 27 acres and with ramparts, in some places five metres high, this was the first, and probably the most important, Iron Age Hillfort to be built in Hampshire. It is claimed to be one of the finest in England. Under excavation, evidence of grain pits, granaries, houses and roads has been discovered. Walking round the ramparts, reading the explanatory notices and taking in the extensive views from its boundaries, is much the best way to appreciate its imposing position and grandeur. The name Danebury is a reminder that these parts were once home to the Danish invaders.

3. Return to the trig. point and retrace your steps to the road junction and the track passed earlier.

4. Turn right along the track. On reaching two metal gates on the right and a gate on the left. Turn left over a stile by the gate onto a fenced path which leads into a field. Follow the left-hand boundary of this huge field. The terrain dips and rises until it seems almost level with Danebury Hill in the background: don't rush, just take your time and enjoy the marvellous 360-degree views. Eventually pass a stile and continue to a stile in the bottom left-hand corner. Cross the stile to a road (A30). Cross over to a stile opposite and continue ahead, with a young plantation on your right, to a stile and a track.

5. Turn left. In 50 metres, a notice on the right explains that Meon Hill was once the location of an Iron Age Settlement: gruesomely, it also says that 10 beheaded skeletons were uncovered during the excavation. In a further 70 metres, at a metal gate on the left, access is allowed into a field: it is part of a conservation plan under which Meon Hill Farm is being managed. From the field there are superb views across the Test Valley and the Hampshire Downland, with Stockbridge straight ahead. Walk

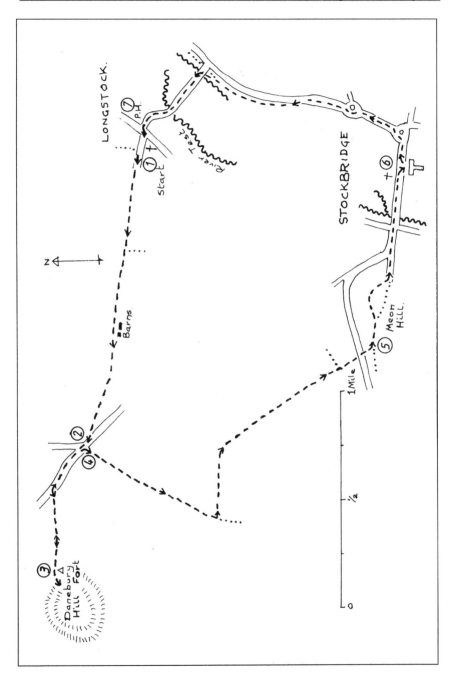

down the field, first going to the left of an electric pylon in order to circle a small, new plantation. Leave the field, near the bottom, by a stile on the right and walk down to the main road. Turn right to walk into Stockbridge.

Sitting contentedly in the beautiful Test Valley, Stockbridge has long been one of the main centres of trout fishing on the River Test. Undisturbed by its transference to the 20th century, the town still retains much of its old-world charm. The Test flows under the wide main street at its western end. Flanked by attractive Tudor and Georgian buildings, the street is further enhanced by a series of channels of the Test which flow through at all angles. At its eastern end is the town's oldest memorial, the chancel of a long demolished 12th century church. Some wall paintings, an ancient communion table and the medieval door with its old door ring can still be seen.

Before the Reformation Act of 1832, Stockbridge was reputed to be the most rotten of all 'rotten boroughs'. Parliamentary candidates are reputed to have paid at least £70 for each vote cast. The Town Hall was given in 1810 as an election bribe. The handsome 19th century Grosvenor Hotel, dominating the street with its huge columns, although built mainly with wealth from fishing and racing, may also have been helped by proceeds from an election bribe.

In its heyday, the town boasted one of the country's finest racecourses. Edward VII, as Prince of Wales, entered the occasional winning horse, and (sometimes accompanied by Lillie Langtrey, hence Lillie's tea room) was a frequent visitor.

6. From the tea room cross over and continue through Stockbridge to the roundabout. Turn left into the Winchester road. At the next roundabout continue ahead towards Andover – although these are busy roads there is a grass verge on the left to walk along. After ½ mile take a track on the left, signposted 'Test Way, Totton and Inkpen Beacon'. Trees either side of the track help to disguise the fact that you are walking parallel to, and only a few metres from, the main road. At a fork, turn left then immediately right to reach a road. Turn left to enjoy a beautiful tranquil walk across tributaries of the Test, pausing for a while as you cross the Test itself, before entering picturesque Longstock village.

The clear waters of the River Test, where one may be lucky enough to spy a sedge-warbler or reed-bunting, and a street of pretty thatched half-timbered cottages, sheltering under a church spire, ensure that Long-stock is one of the most beautiful spots in the Test valley – even the corner pub has a name in keeping with the setting. The name 'Peat Spade' originates from the days when farm labourers were allowed one day off a year, to cut peat for themselves in the surrounding area.

7. Turn left at the inn then right into Church Road to return to your car.

Longstock village

25. Wherwell, Goodworth Clatford & Chilbolton

Route: This walk links three picturesque Test Valley villages and inevitably involves some road walking. For the most part, the route follows undulating fieldpaths, well-made forest tracks, the Rivers Test and Anton, plus one short hill climb. There are excellent views at various stages and a beautiful picnic spot by the Anton at Goodworth Clatford.

Tea shop: **Chestnut Cottage Tea Room** is a charming thatched cottage with a lovely tea room and a delightful cottage garden: in late summer there is a magnificent show of huge colourful hollyhocks. The menu offers a good range of light lunches and delicious home-made cakes and scones. It is open May-October, Wednesday-Sunday, 10.30am-5.30pm. Tel: 01264 860 741.

Distance: 8½ miles.

How to get there: Wherwell is on the B3420, 1½ miles south of Andover.

Public Transport: Bus service: Stagecoach Hampshire Buses.

Start: GR 391408. Wherwell car park, adjacent to the church.

Maps: Landranger 185; Explorer 131; Pathfinders 1222 (SU24/34) and 1242 (SU23/33).

Set in a wooded valley, with the river running through, Wherwell is one of the prettiest villages in the Test Valley. A row of thatched timber-framed cottages by the War Memorial is said to be the most photographed in the county.

The village owes its existence to the Saxon Queen Elfrida, who founded one of the largest medieval religious houses for women in England here. The nunnery was a belated penance for her murder of her stepson Edward so that her own son Ethelred the Unready could take the throne. Previously, she had been party to the murder of her first husband, Earl Ethelwold, by King Edgar, the first King of all England, so that they could marry. Ethelwold had been sent by King Edgar to woo Elfrida on his behalf. Seeing and falling in love with Elfrida, Ethelwold took her for himself in the hope that the King would forget and that Elfrida would never discover the true reason for his visit – it was a vain hope! Today nothing remains of the nunnery: on its site is a handsome 19th century white mansion, 'The Priory'.

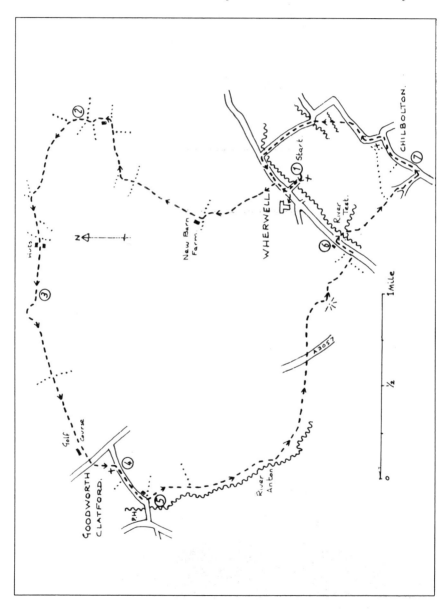

1. From the car park return to the main road. Bear right past the row of thatched cottages. On reaching another row of thatched cottages, one of which is called 'The Forge', turn left along a gravel track to pass through a gate. From the gate, the track becomes part of the Test Way. It first ascends, then descends to New Barn Farm. Cross the farm track and continue along the Test Way, gently ascending to a crossing. Continue ahead, now skirting Harewood Forest on the left with open fields on the right. On reaching a three-way signpost, continue for 100 metres to farm buildings. Here, turn left to descend into the forest.

    It was in Harewood Forest that King Edgar murdered Earl Ethelwold. In the middle of the forest, at a place called Deadman's Plack is a large stone memorial commemorating the murder.

    During the Second World War much of the forest was used as an ammunition store – hence its well-made concrete tracks and derelict Nissen huts.

2. At a crossing track, leave the Test Way and continue ahead. Keep left at a fork. Eventually a crossing path is reached. Here, turn left. Ignore all paths off and keep ahead to reach two corrugated asbestos Nissen huts. Pass between the huts and descend between hedgerows to a field. Follow the left-hand boundary as it ascends for 200 metres to the end of a copse on your left.

3. Turn left through a wide gap in the trees. Keeping the copse on your left, follow it round to its end. Pass through a wide gap in the hedgerow and turn right. Keeping the hedgerow on your right, descend the field. The far-reaching views are to Goodworth Clatford and beyond across the Test Valley. Cross a track and a stile into Hampshire Golf Course. Keeping to a right-hand hedgerow, pass through the golf course to a road. Cross over to a stile then bear left across two paddocks towards the church and a road.

    Goodworth Clatford is as lovely as its name. In Saxon times, when it was known as 'Goda's enclosure', missionary nuns from Wherwell Priory came to the pagan settlement here. Eventually a small Christian community was formed. Today the dominant feature of the village is the 12th century parish church. Displayed in the church is a moving feature of more

recent times. It is a simple wooden cross from the grave, at Flanders, of
Sergeant Charles Tilley – one of 8 men from the village whose names live
on forever on the roll of honour in the church.

4. Turn right along the quiet winding country road until reaching
   Rose Cottage. Turn left just beyond the cottage.

   Before turning left do go to the bridge over the River Anton. Swans,
   coots and mallards all swim alongside the grassy riverside bank and
   pretty wooden footbridges criss-cross its tributaries – it's an ideal picnic spot. Those in need of more substantial refreshment should continue
   to the road junction and the Royal Oak Inn.

5. Fork right along a bridleway through light woodland. Pass
   through a kissing-gate and continue ahead, first alongside cornfields, then through woodland again to emerge at a field. Follow
   the right-hand boundary down the field, passing under electrical
   cables. Continue ahead, between trees, for 35 metres to a metal
   gate into a field. Follow the right-hand boundary to a road
   (A3057). Cross over, pass through a wooden gate and keep ahead
   for a short, steep ascent. At the top of the knoll there are more
   good views across the valley. Bear right, gently ascending to a
   wooden gate, then descending to a gap in the trees. Turn left,
   then immediately right between hedgerows, and gently ascend
   to a large open field. Two contrasting landmarks can be seen
   from this point – Chilbolton church and the radar dish of Chilbolton Observatory. Turn left within the field and follow the
   right-hand boundary round, gently descending to an old railway
   bridge. Pass under the bridge to a road. Turn left along the road.

6. Pass a thatched cottage 'Westmill' and turn right. Cross two footbridges over the Test into Chilbolton Common. This is a delightfully peaceful spot – a place to linger. Snipe, redshank and other
   birds nest here, more than a hundred species of grasses have
   been found on the common. Keep ahead on a well-defined path.
   Cross a metal footbridge and continue to a track. Turn right then
   left to reach the road.

   A diverse mixture of houses and the delightfully named St Mary-the-
   Less, contribute to the charm of Chilbolton. Halfway along Village Street
   is a charming 16th century half-timbered cottage; beside it is the still

Bridge over the River Test at Wherwell

usable old village grindstone. It was bought in 1910, with money left from the celebrations of the coronation of King Edward V, for farmhands to sharpen their scythes and sickles. Many years later it was used for the sheath knives of American Airmen, billeted here during the Second World War. At the north-east end of the street the church, the tiny village green and a row of superb thatched cottages form one of the most delightful of all village scenes. The name of the church is something of a mystery, but it is thought that when the parish church in Andover was dedicated to St Mary in the 14th century, Chilbolton Church, being in the same deanery, had to step down and become St Mary-the-Less.

7. Turn left along Village Street. On reaching the parish church, turn left along Winchester Road. Reach and cross a stile by a red metal gate. The large, white house seen in the distance is 'The Priory'. Bear right to a planked footbridge in the middle of the field. From the bridge, continue to the right for 60 metres to pass through a gap in the hedge. Bear left across a field to a stile to a road (B3420). Turn left for ½ mile to Wherwell and the teashop. The B3420 is very busy and there is no verge, do take care. From the teashop, cross into Church Lane to return to the car park.

26. Whitchurch & Freefolk

Route: A pleasant, easy walk through meadows, along farm tracks and following the meanders of the River Test. There are beautiful views; field scabious and wild poppies flower in abundance throughout the summer.

Tea shop: **The Silk Mill Tea Room** stands on an island on the River Test. It is reached via a small wooden footbridge. Home-made food can be enjoyed whilst listening to, and feeling, the shudder of the water wheel below. In the picturesque riverside garden, mallards and coots wait expectantly for the inevitable scraps. Open Tuesday-Sunday and Bank Holiday Mondays, 10.30am-5.00pm. Tel: 01256 892 065.

Distance: 5 1/4 miles.

How to get there: Whitchurch is 11 miles south of Newbury, 1/2 mile east of the A34 and B3400 junction.

Public Transport: Bus Services: Stagecoach Hampshire Bus, Oakley Buses. Trains: South West Trains.

Start: GR 463478. Public car park (free) adjacent to the Silk Mill, Winchester Street.

Maps: Landranger 185; Explorer 131; Pathfinder 1223 SU44/54.

Situated on the River Test, Whitchurch is a quiet, quaint town. The White Hart Inn still offers a warm welcome to travellers, as it did when the town was an important staging post. Georgian and half-timbered houses line the road which climbs to Newbury.

For hundreds of years the river has provided the source of power for brush-making, paper-making and corn and woollen mills. The history of milling on the site of the Silk Mill dates back to Domesday. The present picturesque mill was built in 1815 as a woollen mill. The weaving of silk started in the 1820s. In 1838, the mill employed 108 workers, 39 of whom were children under the age of thirteen. During the 1970s, silk was produced for academic, legal and ecclesiastical uses; Ottoman silk was provided for 'taking silk'. Whitchurch, incidently, is the home of the former 'Master of the Rolls', Lord Denning.

Cottages at Freefolk

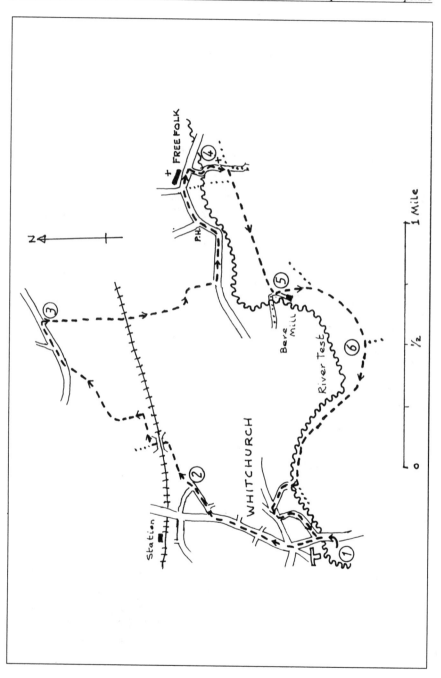

Today the mill is a working museum. It employs five weavers and produces silk for historic houses, interior designers and theatrical costumiers. Recently, two of its most 'famous' orders have been to supply the fringing for the musical *Cats* and bonnet ribbons and silk for gowns for the television production of *Middlemarch*. For further information tel: 01256 892 065.

1. From the car park turn left along Winchester Street, cross the River Test and continue to the roundabout. Turn right into Newbury Street to climb out of the town. Turn right along Dances Lane.

2. On reaching the turning point in the lane, follow a narrow path for 10 metres to a stile into a field. Go diagonally down the field to a stile in the bottom left-hand corner. Turn left, pass under a railway bridge and turn immediately right over a stile into a field. Follow the right-hand boundary down to a stile at the bottom of the field – there is often electric tape here dividing the field. Over the stile keep to the right-hand boundary through this field and a second field to a lane. Turn right along the lane.

3. One hundred and eighty metres beyond the entrance to Wooldings Vineyard, turn right along a grassy track: there is a signpost here but in summer it is almost hidden in the trees. In their seasons, wild flowers blossom prolifically in the hedgerow; in high summer the cornfields on the right are splashed with the scarlet of wild poppies. Eventually cross a railway bridge then descend round a farm on your left to a lane. Turn right to the main road. Turn left along the road for ½ mile to Freefolk.

Freefolk is a small, quiet village, known mainly for its attractive crescent of cottages, its charming 13th century church and more recently, for being the home of Richard Adams – of Watership Down fame. The immaculate row of cottages with thatched roofs, half-timbered gables and long, park-like front gardens, was built in 1939 as almshouses by Lord Portal. St Nicholas is a redundant church, cared for by the Churches Conservation Trust. A minute church, its simple exterior hides a wealth of interest. If you haven't visited the church before, it is best viewed as a surprise.

4. At the end of the crescent of thatched cottages turn right towards
    St Nicholas Church and almost immediately cross a picturesque
    section of the Test. The track passes the church and leads up to a
    cottage. Immediately beyond the cottage turn right through a
    barrier gate into a field. Continue along the top of the field. A
    halfway seat is well placed for admiring the beautiful view
    across the valley. Cross a stile and continue ahead, crossing three
    fields to a house, a lane and an idyllic landscape.

    An 18th century timber-faced mill, a trout-filled river, overhanging willow
    and, in summer, a riot of wild poppies: this scene must have changed lit-
    tle since Cobbett (a passionate opponent of paper money) rode by and
    raged against 'the curse of England'. For it was here in Bere Mill, in the
    1720s, that Henri de Portal, a Huguenot refugee, produced the newly in-
    vented high quality watermarked banknote paper. The industry pros-
    pered and after six years moved to larger premises at nearby
    Laverstoke. Throughout the following years the de Portal family distin-
    guished themselves in service to the county and the country. There is a
    beautiful memorial in honour of the de Portal family in Winchester Cathe-
    dral.

5. Turn left towards the millhouse, then take a fenced footpath
    climbing alongside the garden. Pass through a metal gate into a
    field. Cross up the field, turn right and follow the left-hand
    boundary round to a stile in the bottom right-hand corner.

6. Over the stile, follow a grassy track through a small uncultivated
    area of scrub and trees. Cross a stile and turn right alongside
    fields on your left, occasionally glimpsing the Test through the
    trees on your right. Eventually, a footbridge at Town Mill is
    reached. Cross the bridge, take your fill of yet another pictur-
    esque scene, then continue along the lane, bordered by a tribu-
    tary of the Test, to the road. Turn left then left again into Test
    Road. At the end of the road, cross over to the Silk Mill on the left.

Tea Shop Walks - Spreading everywhere!

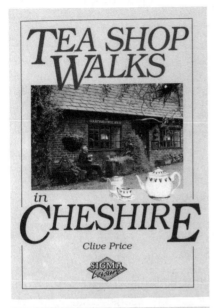

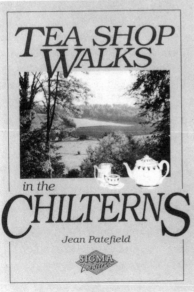

The Sigma Leisure Tea Shop Walks series already includes:

Cheshire

The Chilterns

The Cotswolds

The Lake District, Volume 1

The Lake District, Volume 2

Lancashire

Leicestershire & Rutland

North Devon

The Peak District

Shropshire

Snowdonia

South Devon

Staffordshire

Surrey & Sussex

Warwickshire

The Yorkshire Dales

Each book costs £6.95 and contains a minimum of 25 excellent walks: far better value than any other competitor!

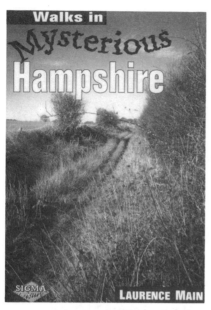

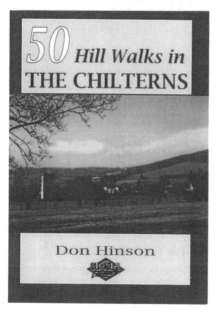